STUDY GUIDE

for use with

FINANCIAL
ACCOUNTING

Robert Libby
Patricia A. Libby
Daniel G. Short

Prepared by
Patricia A. Doherty
Boston University

IRWIN

Chicago · Bogotá · Boston · Buenos Aires · Caracas
London · Madrid · Mexico City · Sydney · Toronto

Printed in the United States of America.

ISBN 0–256–19971–X

3 4 5 6 7 8 9 0 WCB 2 1 0 9 8 7 6

CONTENTS

DO YOU NEED A STUDY GUIDE?

You might well ask. Books are expensive. This one adds to your work load. Do you need it? Think about the subject you are about to study. This is not a "reading" course, where you run through a couple of hundred pages a week. This is a practice and application course. A study guide is meant to save you time, not take up more.

How will this be accomplished? You are introduced in each chapter to new concepts and vocabulary. You are assigned problems that focus your learning. But you cannot successfully solve the problems until you have a fundamental understanding of the concepts. You could read the chapter two or three times, but do you have that much extra time? Here is the value of a Study Guide. In a short order, it covers the major points, as well as the vocabulary, from each chapter. Multiple Choice and True / False exercises are your guide to what you do or do not remember. Sandwiched between reading the chapter, and solution of the longer homework problems, this is your "review." It also serves as a quick refresher before exams.

The more conceptual exercises stretch the basic concepts, giving you short, thought-provoking questions to help you see real-world applications of the procedures. These show you how to apply what you have learned to longer cases and essay-type exam questions.

I hope the Study Guide helps you to complete your accounting course successfully. If you would like to offer any comments on how you used the Study Guide, or suggestions on how it could be more useful, feel free to write to me at

Boston University
School of Management
Department of Accounting
704 Commonwealth Avenue
Boston, MA 02215

1

CHAPTER 1

FINANCIAL STATEMENTS AND BUSINESS DECISIONS

Begin at the beginning, and go on till you come to the end: then stop.

Lewis Carroll

OVERVIEW

Business people need financial information to make rational economic decisions. Investors and creditors need financial information before they provide cash to a business. A primary source of financial information is the organization's financial statements. The primary purpose of this chapter is to describe how the results of business operations are reflected in the numbers in the basic financial statements and how the statements are used, and to introduce the parties involved in the accounting communication process.

LEARNING OBJECTIVES

1. Recognize the information conveyed in the four basic financial statements and how it is used by different decision makers (investors, creditors, and managers).

2. Identify the role of Generally Accepted Accounting Principles in determining the content of financial statements.

3. Distinguish the roles of managers and auditors in the accounting communication process.

4. Appreciate the importance of ethics, reputation, and legal liability in accounting.

CHAPTER OUTLINE

What are we trying to learn in this course?

To understand financial statements

To understand business operations

To understand how financial statements are used in decision making

Who are the people with a financial interest in a business?

Owners, who hope their investment will give them gains from two sources
>   •sale of their investment in the future at more than the purchase price
>
>   •periodic shares of the company's earnings in the form of dividends

Creditors, who gain by charging interest on the money they have loaned the company

Who are the decision makers using accounting information?

External decision makers
>   •creditors and potential investors are external decision makers
>
>   •developing this information is the role of financial accounting

Internal decision makers
>   •the company's managers are internal decision makers
>
>   •the development of this information is the function of managerial accounting

---

Reference point: Exhibit 1 in your text summarizes the roles of financial and managerial accounting, and the users of the information produced by these branches of the accounting system

---

What are the four basic financial statements, and what information does each convey?

The Balance Sheet
>   •the name of the **entity**, or the organization for which we are collecting financial data.
>
>   •the specific date for which this financial position is calculated: a balance sheet is a financial *snapshot*
>
>   •the **monetary unit** of measure used by the entity
>
>   •the financial position of that entity, that is, its *assets*, *liabilities*, and the *owners' equity*.
>>   ◊**assets** are economic resources, expected to provide future benefit, measured at their acquisition cost
>>>   ·not intended to convey market value

3

◊**liabilities** are the various short- and long-term claims against the company's economic resources

·represent one of the sources used to acquire assets

·created by the purchase of goods or borrowing of funds

◊**stockholders'** or **owners' equity** is the amount of financing provided by owners, or the residual claim of owners against assets after creditors (liabilities) have been satisfied

·contributed capital, consisting of cash and other assets invested by owners

·retained earnings, or earnings kept in the business, not distributed as dividends

◊these three items are the elements of the basic *accounting* or **balance sheet equation**

Assets = Liabilities + Equity

The Income Statement

•activity for a specified period of time

•the entity's *revenues*, less the *expenses* incurred in earning those revenues

•*net income = revenue - expenses*

◊net income is also called net earnings, or profit

◊**revenues** are an *inflow* of assets from ongoing operations

·recognized in the period goods or services are sold, not in the period the cash is received

◊**expenses** are an *outflow* of assets, used up to earn revenues

·cost of goods sold is cost to purchase, or make, merchandise sold

·expense is reported in the period in which goods or services are used, not in the period in which cash is disbursed for them

The Statement of Retained Earnings

•ties together the income statement and the balance sheet

•beginning retained earnings + net income - dividends distributed = ending retained earnings

•may be a separate statement, or reported at the end of the income statement

The Statement of Cash Flows

•inflows and outflows of cash for a period, categorized as

◊**operating activities** , or cash flows directly related to the entity's normal business to earn income

◊**investing activities,** related to the purchase or disposal of productive assets such as equipment, vehicles, or investments in other entities' debt or equity

◊**financing activities** , involving the borrowing and repayment of money, or investments by stockholders, or the payment of dividends

What is in the footnotes to financial statements, and why are they worth reading?

Footnotes *supplement* the information in the statements

•descriptions of the accounting rules applied by the entity

•additional detail about a line item

•additional financial disclosure about items not contained in the statements

What are generally accepted accounting principles, and why are they important?

Standard measurement rules are used to convey financial information

•Securities and Exchange Commission **(SEC)** has the power to determine the types of financial information that companies must provide to stockholders

◊privately held companies: stock is not sold to the public at large

◊publicly held companies: stock can be bought and sold by investors on organized markets

•Financial Accounting Standards Board **(FASB)** determines detailed accounting treatment of business practices

•standards vary in other countries, because of economic, cultural, political conditions

•assurance that rules are being followed is provided by

◊managers, in a Report of Management

·assume primary responsibility for information conveyed

·ensure accuracy by

∞maintaining system of internal controls

∞hiring outside independent auditors to verify presentation

∞maintaining an audit committee on board of directors to
review other safeguards

◊independent auditors, in a Report of Independent Auditors

·perform an *audit,* or examination of financial statements

·state their opinion of the fairness of financial statement presentation

Information conveyed in financial statements affects

•selling price of company's stock

•bonus compensation of management and employees

•company's competitive advantage

What is the role of ethics in accounting?

American Institute of Certified Public Accountants **(AICPA)** has a strict code of conduct

•penalties include suspension or even expulsion

•violation may damage reputation and practice

•malpractice liability may result from violation

◊accountants are responsible to all parties affected, even if those parties
were not known to the accountant

•**CPA** is required to remain independent of firm that requests audit

SUPPLEMENT A
TYPES OF BUSINESS ENTITIES

What are the types of business entity?

Sole proprietorship

•business has one owner, often the manager

•business is usually small in size

•owner and business are not separate *legal* entities

•*accounting* still regards owner and business to be separate entities

Partnership

•business has two or more owners

•business can vary in size from very small to very large

•partnership contract specifies agreement between (among) owners

•partners not *legally* separate from business, but the business is a separate
accounting entity

◊each general partner has unlimited legal liability

● **Corporation**

    •business is a separate legal *and* accounting entity

    •owners are *stockholders* or *shareholders*

    •stockholders' (owners') liability limited to their investment

    •business has an indefinite life, independent of owners

    •it is easy transfer of ownership

    •is is easy to raise capital by selling shares to a large number of people

    •this i the dominant form of business in the U.S. in economic terms

    •primary disadvantage is that income is taxed doubly:

        ◊company pays tax on income

        ◊shareholders are taxed on distributed income (dividends)

SUPPLEMENT B
EMPLOYMENT IN THE ACCOUNTING PROFESSION TODAY

What are the employment opportunities for someone who studies accounting?

Public accounting

    •as an individual Certified Public Accountant (**CPA**) or, more commonly, as part of a public accounting firm, rendering service in the areas of

        ◊auditing: attesting to the fairness of presentation of financial data

        ◊management consulting services: providing services related to the design and implementation of accounting systems

        ◊tax services: income tax planning and reporting

Employment by organizations, both profit-making and non-profit

    •CPA, **CMA** (Certified Management Accountant) or **CIA** (Certified Internal Auditor) serve in a variety of business areas, from general accounting through general management and management information systems

    •government accountants serve at any level, from local through international

QUESTIONS AND EXERCISES

Multiple Choice:

Choose the best answer to each question below, and circle the letter in front of that answer. Remember that more than one answer may be true, but only one best answers the question, so you may have to think over some questions carefully.

1. When accountants refer to a "creditor" of a company, they mean someone who
   a. owns the company.
   b. owes the company money.
   c. loaned the company money, or allowed it to buy goods and pay for them later.
   d. has reviewed the company favorably in the business press.
   e. takes care of the company's banking needs.

2. Investors who buy shares, or percentages, of a large corporation hope to gain by
   a. selling the shares in the future for a higher price than their purchase price.
   b. receiving a portion of the company's earnings in the form of dividends.
   c. eventually being hired by the company as a manager.
   d. all of the above.
   e. both (a) and (b) above.

3. All of the following are external decision makers except
   a. a stockholder of the company.
   b. the company's sales manager in charge of the London office.
   c. the loan officer at the local bank.
   d. the company's supplier of merchandise for resale.
   e. an industry analyst at a brokerage firm.

4. Each of the following is one of the four basic financial statements except
   a. the income statement.
   b. the statement of cash flows.
   c. the statement of retained earnings.
   d. the balance sheet.
   e. the bank statement.

5. The statement of financial position is another term for
   a. the income statement.
   b. the statement of cash flows.
   c. the company's bank statement.
   d. the results of today's trading in the company's stock.
   e. the balance sheet.

6. Which of the following items is *not* an asset?
   a. Notes payable
   b. Inventories
   c. Land
   d. Accounts receivable
   e. Cash

7. Amounts owed by customers to the company for prior sales to these customers are contained on the balance sheet as _____ , whereas amounts owed by the company to suppliers for prior purchases are contained in the account _____ .
   a. accounts payable … accounts receivable
   b. cash … cash
   c. accounts receivable … accounts payable
   d. inventories … sales
   e. sales … inventories

8. Assets are usually listed on the balance sheet at
   a. their acquisition cost.
   b. their market value on the balance sheet date.
   c. their market value adjusted for any deterioration from storage.
   d. their cost adjusted for inflation since the purchase date.
   e. their expected selling price.

9. Retained earnings is the amount of

    a. cash that stockholders may reasonably expect to receive as dividends in the future.

    b. earnings held for payment of executive bonuses.

    c. cash left over after all liabilities for the period have been satisfied.

    d. earnings kept, or reinvested, in the business, and thus not paid out as dividends.

    e. cash invested by the owners of the business.

10. An accounting period is

    a. one year, exactly.

    b. one specific date.

    c. any specified time period.

    d. the time required to collect accounts receivable.

    e. the life of the entity.

11. Revenues are recognized on the income statement

    a. in the period in which cash is collected from the customer

    b. in the period in which an order is received from a customer

    c. in the period in which goods or services are actually provided to the customer.

    d. any time the company receives cash.

    e. all of the above.

12. Each of the following is an expense except

    a. the cost of acquiring merchandise that was just sold.

    b. wages of sales staff.

    c. the Vice President's annual bonus.

    d. the cost of a parcel of land acquired for the construction of a new store.

    e. research and development costs on a potential new product.

13. The statement of retained earnings reconciles numerically the relationship between

    a. the income statement and the balance sheet.

    b. sales and cash collected.

    c. beginning and ending cash.

    d. assets and liabilities.

    e. beginning and ending stockholders' equity.

Use the following facts to answer the next four questions:

Downhill Ski Company had the following balances (in no particular order) at the end of 1995:

Cash	$15,000
Sales	500,000
Accounts receivable	300,000
Cost of goods sold	200,000
Land and buildings	1,000,000
Inventories	20,000
Contributed capital	750,000
Dividend paid	15,000
Net income	30,000
Liabilities	?
Operating expenses	?
Retained earnings	?

14. Using the above information, what is the amount of total assets?
    a. $1,335,000
    b. $1,835,000
    c. $2,085,000
    d. $2,615,000
    e. $1,035,000

15. What are total operating (selling and administrative) expenses?
    a. This cannot be determined with the limited information given.
    b. $0
    c. $270,000
    d. $200,000
    e. $20,000

16. Suppose retained earnings had a balance at the beginning of this period of $300,000. What is the balance at the end of this period?

    a. $30,000

    b. $285,000

    c. $345,000

    d. $330,000

    e. $315,000

17. What would total liabilities be at the end of the period, given all of the above?

    a. Cannot be calculated, since no liability amounts are given.

    b. $0

    c. $1,335,000

    d. $270,000

    e. $2,700,000

18. Even though a company produces an income statement and balance sheet that show activity in and balances of all the company's accounts, they also have to produce a statement of cash flows because

    a. the items on the income statement have nothing to do with cash.

    b. the amount of cash shown on the balance sheet is not necessarily current and accurate.

    c. net income is not necessarily equal to cash generated by the company.

    d. it is often useful to look at the same items in more than one way.

    e. it is needed to reconcile the income statement to the balance sheet.

19. The statement of cash flows is divided into the following categories:

    a. cash inflows, cash outflows.

    b. current, non-current.

    c. operating, investing, financing.

    d. assets, liabilities, equity.

    e. revenues, expenses.

20. Footnotes to financial statements
    a. describe accounting rules applied in the preparation of the attached statements.
    b. present additional detail about particular line items.
    c. present information about items not listed in the financial statements themselves.
    d. all of the above.
    e. are optional, and present any information the company wishes to append to its statements.

True or False?

For each of the following statements, place the letter **"T"** or **"F"** in the space before the statement to indicate whether you think the statement is true or false. Remember to think about *why* each statement you mark with an "F" is false, and try to re-word the statement to make it true, to be sure you understand the concept.

_____ 21. The managers of a company are always required to have some financial stake in—that is, they must *own* a portion of—that company.

_____ 22. The focus of financial accounting is on external users, whereas the focus of managerial accounting is on internal users of accounting information.

_____ 23. The balance sheet is prepared to reflect activities over a specified period of time, such as one year.

_____ 24. The accounting, or balance sheet, equation states that Assets + Liabilities = Equity.

_____ 25. An item is considered to be an expense as soon as, but not before, the company has paid out cash for it.

_____ 26. The FASB specifies the laws under which financial statements are prepared, and the SEC enforces these laws.

_____ 27. The FASB actively solicits the input of the business community in the development of new accounting rules.

_____ 28. A company's internal control procedures guarantee that no errors will slip into their books of account or their published financial statements.

_____ 29. A partnership or a sole proprietorship is characterized legally by unlimited liability, that is, the owner is personally liable for the debts of the business. This is not true of a corporation.

_____ 30. In an accounting sense, a corporation is a separate entity from its owners, but this is not true of partnerships or sole proprietorships.

A Few Words from You ...

Answer each of the following with a short discussion (a paragraph will cover it) of the issues involved.

31. **Who needs a CPA?** Your text notes that many accountants, including CPAs, work in private industry. Explain why a *private* company would find a person who was a Certified *Public* Accountant a desirable employee.

32. **What do the numbers mean?** You have learned that assets are reported on the balance sheet at their original cost. Why do you think this is done? What are the advantages of this practice? What are the disadvantages?

33. **Why is this an asset?** Accounts receivable are classified as an asset. How can something you do not have yet be an asset?

34. **Why should a company retain any earnings?** Retained earnings were defined for you as accumulated earnings of an entity kept in the business, and thus not distributed as dividends. Suppose a company decides to distribute *all* of its earnings each year as dividends. Will the stockholders welcome this decision? Would *you*, if you were a stockholder? Why or why not?

35. **Can you afford unlimited liability?** Owners of partnerships and sole proprietorships are personally liable for the obligations of their businesses. What could you as an owner do to protect your personal assets and yet fairly treat the creditors of your business?

Team up!

Get together in teams of 3 - 5 members to decide each of the following:

36. **What goes on a balance sheet?** Anyone can have a balance sheet, you don't have to be a company. Come up with a list of items that would be on the balance sheet of a typical college student. What are your assets? What are your liabilities? How would you determine your "equity?" You can attach approximate or hypothetical values, so that you do not have to go too far into anyone's personal finances. Put your balance sheet into a form similar to Exhibit 2 in your text. (Obviously you will not have the equity structure of a corporation. Just use one line, called "equity.")

37. **How are we going to fix this?** You have read through the entire Maxidrive case, and been made aware of their deficiencies in accounting and reporting. What would it be like to be a member of a management team that had to report what happened to the stockholders?

Choose one team, or select members from more than one team, to prepare a presentation for the rest of your class on this case. The presenters will take the roles of members of the company and its support team: the internal management (perhaps an officer, someone in charge of the internal control system, and the internal auditor), a representative or two from the outside auditors, and someone from the Board of Directors' audit committee. This "management committee" must come up with an explanation of the disaster, and a "damage control" plan. They will then present this package to the rest of the class, who will represent the understandably concerned and angry stockholders, who will have the opportunity to question the presenters.

17

38. **Let's go into business together!** Pretend you and your team members are going to start a small business as partners. Decide what kind of business it will be, and draw up a partnership agreement, including what you believe will be necessary to run the business smoothly, and protect everyone's interests. Once these agreements are finished, you might exchange them with other teams, and "troubleshoot" each other's agreements, pointing out deficiencies and offering suggestions for improvement.

And just for the fun of it ...

The following matrix contains the names of all of the basic financial statements, including alternate names for two of them, and the principal subdivisions of each statement. Can you find them?

```
S T A S R T S M S S O R P N A D F W I L S B E R S T D R T E
E V A D E N S R P E A I C L I B I E N N E E I T I S A W Y M
S I C U V A Y M F I S I S U P E R C S A L F R A G I L I S T
I E X P E I A L I D S T A T E M E N T O F C A S H F L O W S
B E G I N N I N G R E T A I N E D E A R N I N G S O C I O G
U S A N U I I O D I T S E S T A B L T I S H M E N T A R I N
A N I S E M E P P I S P H E N O M I E N A L L Y L Y M P E I
M N E A S R U E B C H D F G H W I J M A O E I P R S O H N N
Y E U R O E P R T H E L I I N C O M E S T A T E M E N T D R
X E D E M A T A O U S H A T H U E K N V W I Y U Z H N O I A
L I A B I L I T I E S X L D O G C L T R O G V B W I O G N E
A C N E G I N I R S H O N E T I N C O M E R P G M J C R G D
A U N V T K G N A E R Q B A H N H M F O F E U N X K H A R E
U T E R E M A G M D E U N L I N D N F E N P Q L P E R P E N
S S S T R S I O O A S I E G E M T E I I N S E U L M O H T I
G E E M E O T I N S C N H A F E T E N N B A D E I C M I A A
B L S L S G C I H A F N T A E N Z U A Z Y T I C I T A C I T
U G N G O Q E T N T E R D H A M M E N R U N G A H I Y O N E
T R E Q C U T C H G I P S E M L A G C O D I O R I B E N E R
T R P E M S I F A S D E L L A E T I I D D E M E T E R R D F
E O X E O G I E Y D C O M A S H N C A E D G K T D A N C E O
R Y E F Z U I T O N D P Y F U D L C L V H J L Z A P P Y A T
S C A P I W S T A T E M E N T O F O P E R A T I O N S P R N
C C A I A N O L E L E E L Y G R A W O I O H A P P Y D Y N E
O I E R T Y A P M E P A T T I A T R S T N S Y I F Q R Z I M
T F R A P B L N E N T A R Y M Z S A I A Z C D Z H L N E N E
C T G U E B D I C L A R K E X Y D E T R X Q O M L D Q M G T
H D S I I D A E X I C U L V D N E D I V I D D I H E H C S A
X A C Y S F H J L N N B T P A T O R O E F D B X Y Z B O M T
S C U P P E R S M P R G M U I A H Y N F I L O R P O L E Y S
```

19

SOLUTIONS

Multiple Choice

1. (c) 2. (e) 3. (b) 4. (e) 5. (e) 6. (a) 7. (c) 8. (a) 9. (d) 10. (c) 11. (c) 12. (d) 13. (a) 14. (a) 15. (c) 16. (e) 17. (d) 18. (c) 19. (c) 20. (d)

True or False?

21. False. Managers may, but do not necessarily have to, be owners of a company.

22. True

23. False. The balance sheet is prepared as of one specific date.

24. False. The accounting equation states that Assets = Liabilities + Equity. Therefore, transposing this equation to a form similar to this problem, Assets *minus* (not plus) liabilities would equal equity.

25. False. Expense is recognized when an asset us used up in the earning of revenue, independent of when cash is exchanged.

26. False. The SEC regulates what companies must report to their owners. The FASB determines the details of the accounting treatment of various business transactions. The FASB pronouncements are accounting conventions or practices, not laws.

27. True.

28. False. A good internal control system minimizes errors or deliberate deception. No system can totally prevent these things.

29. True.

30. False. All three are separate *accounting* entities. Only a corporation is a separate *legal* entity.

And just for the fun of it ...

```
S T A S R T S M S S O R P N A D F W I L S B E R S T D R T E
E V A D E N S R P E A I C L I B I E N N E E I T I S A W Y M
S I C U V A Y M F I S I S U P E R C S A L F R A G I L I S T
I E X P E I A L I D S T A T E M E N T O F C A S H F L O W S
B E G I N N I N G R E T A I N E D E A R N I N G S O C I O G
U S A N U I I O D I T S E S T A B L T I S H M E N T A R I N
A N I S E M E P P I S P H E N O M I E N A L L Y L M P E I
M N E A S R U E B C H D F G H W I J M A O E I P R S O H N N
Y E U R O E P R T H E L I I N C O M E S T A T E M E N T D R
X E D E M A T A O U S H A T H U E K N V W I Y U Z H N O I A
L I A B I L I T I E S X L D O G C L T R O G V B W I O G N E
A C N E G I N I R S H O N E T I N C O M E R P G M J C R G D
A U N V T K G N A E R Q B A H N H M F O F E U N X K H A R E
U T E R E M A G M D E U N L I N D N F E N P Q L P E R P E N
S S S T R S I O O A S I E G E M T E I I N S E U L M O H T I
G E E M E O T I N S C N H A F E T E N N B A D E I C M I A A
B L S L S G C I H A F N T A E N Z U A Z Y T I C I T A C I T
U G N G O Q E T N T E R D H A M M E N R U N G A H I Y O N E
T R E Q C U T C H G I P S E M L A G C O D I O R I B E N E R
T R P E M S I F A S D E L L A E T I I D D E M E T E R R D F
E O X E O G I E Y D C O M A S H N C A E D G K T D A N C E O
R Y E F Z U I T O N D P Y F U D L C L V H J L Z A P P Y A T
S C A P I W S T A T E M E N T O F O P E R A T I O N S P R N
C C A I A N O L E L E E L Y G R A W O I O H A P P Y D Y N E
O I E R T Y A P M E P A T T I A T R S T N S Y I F Q R Z I M
T F R A P B L N E N T A R Y M Z S A I A Z C D Z H L N E N E
C T G U E B D I C L A R K E X Y D E T R X Q O M L D Q M G T
H D S I I D A E X I C U L V D N E D I V I D D I H E H C S A
X A C Y S F H J L N N B T P A T O R O E F D B X Y Z B O M T
S C U P P E R S M P R G M U I A H Y N F I L O R P O L E Y S
```

CHAPTER 2

THE ACCOUNTING MODEL AND TRANSACTION ANALYSIS

Now go, write it before them in a table, and note it in a book.

Old Testament, Isaiah xxx.8

OVERVIEW

In Chapter 1, we learned the basic financial statements which communicate financial information to external users. Chapters 2, 3, and 4 provide a more detailed look at financial statements and examine how the accounting function translates data about business transactions into these statements. Learning how to translate back and forth between business transactions and financial statements is the key to the use of financial statements in planning and decision making. In Chapter 2 we begin our discussions of how the accounting function collects data about business transactions and how those data are processed to provide the periodic financial statements, with emphasis on the balance sheet. The chapter discusses key accounting concepts, the accounting model, transaction analysis, and analytical tools. We will examine typical business activities of an actual service-oriented company to demonstrate the concepts in Chapters 2, 3, and 4.

LEARNING OBJECTIVES

1. Define the objective of financial reporting, the elements of the balance sheet, and the related key accounting assumptions and principles.

2. Identify what constitutes a business transaction.

3. Define an account and identify common balance sheet account titles used in business.

4. Apply transaction analysis to analyze simple business transactions in terms of the accounting model: Assets = Liabilities + Stockholders' Equity.

5. Record the results of transaction analysis using two basic tools: (a) journal entries and (b) T-accounts.

6. Prepare a simple balance sheet.

CHAPTER OUTLINE

Reference point: Chapter 2 begins a discussion, to be continued in Chapters 3, 4, and 5, of the conceptual "framework" of accounting. Exhibit 1 in your text summarizes this framework. You might want to make a copy of this exhibit, and refer to it as you read these chapters and future chapters. Even if you do not completely understand the exhibit right now, it will provide a useful point of reference as you study new concepts, so that you do not become confused about how new items fit into what you have learned previously. As you finish the five chapters, the exhibit's value as a summary will become clear.

What is the primary objective of financial reporting?

Provide useful economic information

Enable external parties to make decisions about the company

What are some of the assumptions that define the scope and expectations of financial reporting?

Separate-entity assumption accounts for a business separately from its owners, and from all other entities

Unit-of-measure assumption says that a business reports its results in the monetary unit (currency) of its home country

Continuity, or **going-concern** principle, assumes that the business will continue to operate into the foreseeable future

What are the basic elements of a balance sheet?

Assets are items from which the entity expects to derive future economic benefit
- they result from past transactions
- they are usually listed in order of liquidity

Liabilities are debts or obligations of the entity
- they result from past transactions
- entities to whom the debts are owed are called *creditors*
- they are listed in order of maturity

Stockholders' (Owners') Equity is financing provided by the owners or the operations of the entity

•*contributed capital* is cash or other assets contributed by owners

◊owners hope to gain dividends or increase in value of investment

•*retained earnings* are earnings reinvested in entity, not distributed to owners as dividends

What is the cost principle?

An asset is initially recorded on the balance sheet at its original (historical) cost, including cash plus non-cash considerations

What is a business transaction?

A **transaction** is an event with economic impact, recorded as part of the accounting process

•external events involve exchanges of assets and liabilities between entity and other parties

•internal events do not involve outside parties but are adjustments made because they have a measurable effect on the entity

•some events, even though they have economic impact, do not involve exchanges of assets or liabilities and are thus not recorded

What is an account?

An **account** is a way of accumulating the dollar effects of transactions on a single element of a financial statement

•chart of accounts lists all the entity's accounts

•accounts are organized by financial statement element

•financial statement accounts may actually be summations of a number of accounts in the entity's books

•types of accounts vary by the type of business the entity is engaged in

How do transactions affect accounts?

Transaction analysis studies the effect of a transaction on the basic accounting equation:

$$Assets = Liabilities + Equity$$

•remember this is an algebraic equation, so that

◊any transaction affects the equation in at least two accounts (**duality of effect**)

·entity gives up something, and receives something in return

◊the equation must be kept in balance at all times

24

•thus transaction analysis involves the following steps

◊identify accounts affected (at least two, possibly more), classified as asset, liability or equity

◊determine amount of increase (+) or decrease (-) in each account

◊make sure equation is still in balance after these effects are recorded

---

Reference point: At this point go back to your textbook and carefully review the transactions (A - F) analyzed for you. Make sure you have completed transactions G through J yourself, to be certain you understand transaction analysis.

What are the actual mechanics of transaction analysis?

•an increase is written on the *left* side of an account when the account is on the *left* side of the equation (that is, when the account is an *asset*)

◊the *left* side of an account is called the *debit* side

•an increase is written on the *right* side of an account when the account is on the *right* side of the equation (that is, when it is a *liability* or an *equity* account)

◊the *right* side of an account is called the *credit* side

•thus *assets* have *debit* balances, and *liabilities* and *equity* have *credit* balances

•debit and credit mean no more than left and right, respectively

•total value of all debits in a transaction should equal total dollar value of all credits

How do actual companies record transactions to keep track of account balances?

A **journal entry** records a transaction as it occurs

•debits written first

•credits follow below debits, indented to the right

•if more than two accounts are affected, it is called a *compound* entry

•entries are recorded in chronological order in a book called a *journal*

T-accounts summarize journal entries by account and determine account balances

•dollar amounts recorded in accounts are posted (transferred) from the journal to a ledger

•ledger is kept by account

◊debits recorded as usual on left of each account, credits on right

•T-account is a simplified ledger account

◊it is shaped as its name implies

◊debits are recorded on the left of any account, and credits on the right

---

Reference point: Work carefully through the illustrated journal entries in your text to understand the proper use of journal entries and T-accounts. Pay close attention to transactions G through J, which you are expected to complete yourself. In future chapters it will be assumed that you can analyze, journalize and post transactions. Make sure now that you have a clear understanding of the basic model.

QUESTIONS AND EXERCISES

Multiple Choice:

Choose the best answer to each question below, and circle the letter in front of that answer. Remember that more than one answer may be true, but only one best answers the question, so you may have to think over some questions carefully.

1. Providing external parties with economic information about a business so that they can make sound financial decisions is the primary objective of

    a. the *Wall Street Journal*.

    b. external financial reporting.

    c. news releases.

    d. financial analysts.

    e. external auditors.

2. The separate-entity concept maintains that a business must be accounted for separately from

    a. its owners and all other persons or entities.

    b. other business entities only.

    c. other related businesses.

    d. its owners.

    e. its owners only if it is a corporation, but not if it is a partnership or proprietorship.

3. The continuity, or going-concern, assumption holds that a business will continue to operate

    a. forever.

    b. for at least the length of the current fiscal year.

    c. long enough to meet contractual commitments and plans.

    d. for the life (lives) of its owners.

    e. as long as it remains profitable.

4. Recently a number of automobile manufacturers published recalls of auto models containing seat belts that might fail under stress. The anticipated cost to the auto manufacturers for replacing these seat belts should

    a. not be recorded because it cannot be precisely calculated.

    b. be recorded as a liability because it is probable and can be reasonably estimated.

    c. be ignored under the assumption that most of the cars are old, and if the belts have not failed up to now they probably will not do so; thus consumers are unlikely to go to the trouble of having the seat belts replaced.

    d. be recorded only when someone actually brings in a car and requests the replacement.

    e. be recorded as an accrued asset, then expensed when replacements actually are made.

5. An event with an economic impact on the entity, that is recorded as part of the accounting process, is known as a(n)

    a. account.

    b. external event.

    c. exchange.

    d. asset.

    e. transaction.

6. A transaction that is an external event involves

    a. an exchange of assets and liabilities between the business and one or more other parties.

    b. any event that happens outside of the business.

    c. any event that occurs outside the principal location of the business.

    d. anything involving persons not owning or employed by the business.

    e. any event that has an economic impact on the entity.

7. When we speak in accounting of the *duality of effects* , we mean that

    a. there is more than one way of looking at any situation.

    b. there are two entities involved in every transaction.

    c. every transaction affects at least two accounts.

    d. every transaction must be recorded twice.

    e. every transaction has both a good and a bad aspect.

The following three questions will ask you to analyze some transactions that McDonald's might typically encounter. McDonald's is a leading food service retailer in the global marketplace, with nearly 13,100 outlets in 65 countries as of their 1992 annual report.

8. When McDonald's purchases paper cups on 30 days' credit from a supplier, they receive _____ and give up _____.
     a. inventory; cash
     b. inventory; accounts payable
     c. accounts payable; cash
     d. inventory; accounts receivable
     e. accounts payable; accounts receivable

9. When after 30 days McDonald's pays the supplier for the paper cups they received, they would
     a. decrease an asset
     b. decrease a liability
     c. decrease an asset and increase a liability
     d. decrease a liability and increase an asset
     e. both (a) and (b) above

10. McDonald's buys a new microwave oven, giving the dealer a $200 down payment, and signing a promissory note agreeing the pay the $800 balance in 60 days. One account would _____ and two others would _____. These accounts are, respectively, _____ and _____, _____.
     a. decrease, increase. cash, equipment, notes payable
     b. increase, decrease. cash, equipment, notes payable
     c. decrease, increase. notes payable, equipment, cash
     d. increase, decrease. equipment, notes payable, cash
     e. increase, increase. equipment, accounts receivable, accounts payable

11. A company records journal entries in _____ order.
   a. alphabetical
   b. account
   c. no particular
   d. chronological
   e. balance sheet

12. Increases to accounts on the left side of the accounting equation are recorded on the _____; increases to accounts on the right side of the accounting equation are recorded on the _____.
   a. left; right
   b. left; left
   c. right; left
   d. right; right
   e. all of the above could be correct under different circumstances.

13. A journal entry which affects more than two accounts is called a
   a. double entry.
   b. general journal.
   c. special journal.
   d. compound entry.
   e. internal entry.

14. A T-account is a simplified form of a
   a. journal entry.
   b. balance sheet.
   c. ledger account.
   d. purchase order.
   e. customer invoice.

Let's go back to McDonald's Corp. A simplified version of the Balance Sheet found in their December 31, 1992 Annual Report follows:

($millions)

Current assets:

Cash and equivalents	$436.5	
Accounts receivable	245.9	
Notes receivable	33.7	
Inventories	43.5	
Prepayments & other current assets	105.1	
Total current assets		$864.7

Other assets and deferred charges:

Notes receivable	99.0	
Investments in & advances to affiliates	399.7	
Miscellaneous	330.7	
Total other assets & deferred charges		829.4
Property and equipment, net		9,597.4
Intangible assets, net		389.7
Total assets		**$11,681.2**

Current liabilities:

Notes payable	$411.0	
Accounts payable	343.3	
Income taxes	109.7	
Other taxes	74.8	
Accrued interest	133.3	
Other accrued liabilities	203.1	
Current maturities of long-term debt	269.4	
Total current liabilities		1,544.6

Long-term debt		3,176.4
Security deposits of franchisees, other		225.2
Deferred income taxes		748.6
Common stock put options		94.0
Total liabilities		5,788.8

Preferred stock	680.2	
Common stock	46.2	
Additional paid-in capital	260.2	
Guarantee of ESOP notes	(271.3)	
Retained earnings	6727.3	
Foreign currency translation adjustment	(127.4)	
	7315.2	
Common stock in treasury, at cost	(1422.8)	
Total stockholders' equity		5,892.4
Total liabilities and equity		**$11,681.2**

Use this balance sheet to answer the next four questions. For each one, assume that no other transactions have taken place.

15. The purchase of $.5 mil of beef on credit would result in the following entry:
     a. debit to inventory, credit to cash of $.5 mil
     b. debit to accounts receivable, credit to cash of $.5 mil
     c. debit to inventory, credit to accounts payable of $.5 mil
     d. debit to inventory, debit to accounts payable of $.5 mil
     e. credit to inventory, credit to cash of $.5 mil

16. After the entry in problem 15 (above), total assets would be
     a. $11,681.7
     b. $11,681.2
     c. $11,680.7
     d. $11,682.2
     e. $11,680.2

17. After McDonald's pays the supplier for the beef, the balance of assets will be _____ and the balance of liabilities and equity will be _____.
     a. $11,681.2; 11,681.2
     b. $11,681.7; $11,681.7
     c. $11,681.7; $11,681.2
     d. $11,681.2; $11,681.7
     e. $11,680.7; $11,680.7

18. Suppose McDonald's collects $2.5 mil that was owed to it by franchisees. The proper entry to record the collection would be:

     a. Accounts payable   2.5
            Accounts receivable   2.5

     b. Accounts receivable   2.5
            Cash   2.5

     c. Cash   2.5
            Inventory   2.5

     d. Cash   2.5
            Accounts receivable   2.5

     e. Cash   2.5
            Accounts payable   2.5

19. Consider the following hypothetical T-account for McDonald's Corp.(taken in part from actual balance sheet amounts):

Accounts Receivable		
beginning balance	238.4	
sales on account	7133.3	
		??
ending balance	245.9	

The missing amount of $_____ represents _____.

    a. $7125.8; total sales

    b. $7125.8; collections on account from credit customers

    c. $7617.6; collections on account from credit customers

    d. $7617.6; total sales

    e. $245.9; total accounts receivable

20. McDonald's balance sheet [see exhibit before question (15)] lists a group of "current liabilities," then some additional liabilities that could be called "non-current liabilities." A non-current liability (such as long-term debt) is one which

    a. was a liability in the past, but is no longer one.

    b. will be a liability someday, but need not be a concern now.

    c. the company does not expect to fully pay off within the coming year.

    d. is larger than a current liability.

    e. all of the above.

True or False?

In the space before each statement, place the letter "T" or "F" to indicate whether the statement is true or false. Rewrite each false statement, making it true, to assure your understanding of the concept.

_____ 21. In accounting, we often refer to asset acquisition activities as financing activities.

_____ 22. The balance sheet shows an entity's assets and how they were acquired; revenues and their related expenses are shown on the income statement.

_____ 23. Liabilities are recorded on the balance sheet when they are probable, and can be reasonably estimated.

_____ 24. When we refer to "contributed capital" in the stockholders' equity section of the balance sheet, we mean money that has been given outright to the firm with no expectation of a return on these funds.

_____ 25. Sometimes important events with an economic impact on the entity are not recorded in the entity's financial statements.

_____ 26. Assets are recorded at cost based on an arm's-length exchange with an external party; thus the balance sheet will always reflect the market value of assets.

_____ 27. A company's published balance sheet will often aggregate a number of its detailed accounts onto one line for simplicity of presentation.

_____ 28. The accounting equation must remain in balance in total, but it is not necessary to keep it in balance after every transaction is recorded.

_____ 29. Transactions must be measured precisely and objectively, so that reported accounting results reflect exactly what happened during a period.

_____ 30. The recording and reporting of economic transactions often requires considerable professional judgment on the part of the accountant, not simply a repetition of facts.

A few words from you ...

Answer each of the following with a short discussion (a paragraph will do) of the issues involved, or a calculation, or both.

31. Complete the following chart of the debit / credit rules by filling in the correct word—debit or credit—in each blank:

	ASSETS	LIABILITIES	EQUITY
INCREASE			
DECREASE			
USUAL BALANCE			

Explain why an increase in assets is accomplished by the same device as a decrease in equity. Isn't this illogical?

32. **Are there assets that we don't see on the balance sheet?** An article in *The Wall Street Journal* in June of 1995[1] discussed the proposed acquisition of Lotus Development Corp. by IBM Corp. The article contained the following:

> Hostile runs at software companies were deemed all but undoable in the 1980s because the real assets—the creative minds who found such companies and crunch the programming code—could simply walk out the door. IBM clearly runs that risk. Notes's chief designer, Raymond Ozzie, is an iconoclast who might leave, along with a number of others, if IBM's bid succeeds, contends Karl Wong, an analyst at Dataquest. "IBM could be buying a shell of a company. Ray Ozzie isn't an IBM-mold type employee," he says. Mr Ozzie couldn't be reached for comment.

Explain what Mr. Wong means when he refers to "a shell of a company." Will there be no assets on the Lotus balance sheet?

---

[1]Hays, Laurie, Steven Lipin and William M. Bulkeley, "Software Landscape Shifts as IBM Makes Hostile Bid for Lotus," *The Wall Street Journal* , June 6, 1995, p.1.

33. **How do real companies use the concepts we've covered in transaction analysis?** Refer to Multiple Choice question number (4). Suppose you work for an automobile manufacturer who installed the seat belts, now considered defective, in its automobiles in the past. Your employer has decided that the company must issue a recall of the cars in question and offer to replace the seat belts for the owners free of charge. How would you go about determining the potential cost to your company? Use transaction analysis to determine how you would record the potential effect of this recall on your company. Assume that no repairs have been done yet. Your company just wants to record its probable exposure.

> (a) Identify the accounts affected. You do not need to know special names for the accounts. Give them names that seem logical to you. Are they assets, liabilities or equity accounts?
>
> (b) Which accounts increase and which decrease?
>
> (c) Explain in general terms the effect on the company's balance sheet.

34. **Why is everything written down twice?** Explain the benefit to an entity of maintaining two separate books of account, a journal and a ledger, to record the same transactions.

35. **Why is the continuity assumption important?** Suppose that you were told that a company whose balance sheet you were analyzing would only be in business for the remainder of this year; that is, that the continuity assumption does not hold for this company. How might this change your opinion of the statement? On which accounts in particular would you focus your attention? You could use the Sbarro Balance Sheet (Exhibit 5 in your text) as an example in choosing accounts).

Team up!

Get together in teams of 3 - 5 members to decide each of the following.

36. **Some transactions for a small business.** You will be checking one another's work for this exercise, so you will want to begin the first part in smaller teams—in pairs.

a. Lisa and Charley operate a yacht maintenance service. They work out of their home, their own yacht "Odyssey." At the beginning of a new season, they did the following:

  1) They purchased a new outboard motor for their small inflatable launch for $4500, giving the dealer a $500 down payment and a promissory note for the remainder, to be paid in 4 monthly installments beginning in 30 days.
  2) They purchased $850 of supplies to be used in their business from the local chandlery on open account.
  3) They transferred $1,000 from their personal savings account into the checking account of the business (the business is incorporated as "Odyssey, Inc.").
  4) They paid the chandlery $200 cash to run a small ad for their business in the monthly circular that the chandlery's owner mails to customers and business associates during the summer season (the first circular will be mailed in a month).
  5) During the winter Lisa and Charley delivered a yacht to Florida for a customer, and had mailed an invoice to the customer, which was recorded properly on their books of account at the time. When they arrived at the chandlery, the customer's check for $500 was waiting there for them. (They receive their mail through the chandlery.)

Before any of these transactions was recorded, the business had the following accounts and balances, in alphabetical order. Assume that accounts carry their normal (debit or credit) balance.

Accounts receivable	$500
Cash	600
Computer and peripherals, net	4,000
Contributed capital	7,000
Inflatable launch, net	4,000
Retained earnings	2,180
Supplies on hand	80

First, working in pairs, analyze each of the transactions above (1 - 5). For each, identify the accounts involved; whether they are assets, liabilities or equity; the increases and decreases; and the amounts.

Accounts	A, L, or E?	+ or -	Amount

1)

2)

3)

4)

5)

b) Now team up with another pair, forming a group of four. Compare analyses. Do you agree? If not, discuss your reasoning, and decide which analysis is correct for the transactions that differ. Prepare journal entries for each transaction, then post your entries to T-accounts. Before you post the new transactions to the T-accounts, you may want to record their beginning balances, given to you above.

Entries:

1)

2)

3)

4)

5)

T-accounts:

c) Now merge with another group of four. Compare results again. Do you agree on the entries and postings? Remember that your accounts do not have to have precisely the same names. Every company uses its own account titles. Resolve any disagreements by using the transaction analysis model. Now prepare a revised balance sheet for Odyssey, Inc., for April 30, 1995, using the form below.

Odyssey, Inc.
Balance Sheet
at April 30, 1995

ASSETS

$ ____

LIABILITIES

____

OWNERS' EQUITY

____

$ ____

37. **What kinds of accounts do companies use?** List four different types of company. Choose specific examples in a number of categories: a service company (a travel agent, a utility); a manufacturer (automobiles, paper, clothing); a retailer (groceries); local government. For each one, discuss the accounts you would expect the company to have on its chart of accounts. Which accounts are the same? Which are different? Why?

38. **Why do balance sheet accounts change?** Shown below are balance sheets for McDonald's Corp. for the years ended December 31, 1992 and 1991. Compare these balance sheets. What do you think happened to change each account shown? For example, what sorts of transactions could make property and equipment increase? Were there only increases to this account during the year, or a combination of increases and decreases? What might the decreases be?

Try to analyze each account shown in this way. As an interested observer, are any of the changes particularly noteworthy to you? Why? How do you think an outsider could go about finding more information about these? Are some accounts totally unfamiliar to you?

($millions)

	1992	1991
Current assets:		
Cash and equivalents	$436.5	220.2
Accounts receivable	245.9	238.4
Notes receivable	33.7	36.0
Inventories	43.5	42.6
Prepaid expenses & other current	105.1	108.8
Total current assets	864.7	646.0
Other assets and deferred charges:		
Notes receivable	99.0	123.1
Investments in & advances to affiliates	399.7	374.2
Miscellaneous	330.7	278.2
Total other assets & deferred charges	829.4	775.5
Property and equipment, net	9597.4	9558.5
Intangible assets, net	389.7	369.1
Total assets	$11,681.2	$11,349.1
Current liabilities:		
Notes payable	$411.0	278.3
Accounts payable	343.3	313.9
Income taxes	109.7	157.2
Other taxes	74.8	82.3
Accrued interest	133.3	185.7
Other accrued liabilities	203.1	201.4
Current maturities of long-term debt	269.4	69.1
Total current liabilities	1544.6	1287.9
Long-term debt	3176.4	4267.4
Security deposits of franchisees, other	225.2	224.5
Deferred income taxes	748.6	734.2
Common stock put options	94.0	-
Preferred stock	680.2	298.2
Common stock	46.2	46.2
Additional paid-in capital	260.2	201.9
Guarantee of ESOP notes	(271.3)	(286.7)
Retained earnings	6727.3	5925.2
Foreign currency translation adjustment	(127.4)	32.3
	7315.2	6217.1
Common stock in treasury, at cost	(1422.8)	(1382.0)
Total stockholders' equity	5892.4	4835.1
Total liabilities and equity	$11,681.2	$11,349.1

42

● **And just for the fun of it ...**

Accounting trivia:

Whose idea was this anyway? Do you know how long "double entry accounting" has been around? Who invented it or was given credit for doing so? Do you think it is a twentieth century phenomenon? A product of the Industrial Revolution?

SOLUTIONS

Multiple Choice:

1. (b) 2. (a) 3. (c) 4. (b) 5. (e) 6. (a) 7. (c) 8. (b) 9. (e) 10. (a) 11. (d) 12. (a) 13. (d) 14. (c) 15. (c) 16. (a) 17. (a) 18. (d) 19. (b) 20. (c)

True or False?

21. False. Asset acquisitions are investing activities.

22. True.

23. True.

24. False. Even though there is the suggestion of a "donation" in the word *contributed*, it is not so. All amounts invested in the entity by its owners are called contributed capital, and contributors expect dividends and/or a gain in the value of their investment.

25. True.

26. False. Assets are recorded at their historical cost at acquisition. As time passes their market value may deviate from this value, without necessarily causing a corresponding change in the balance sheet amount.

27. True

28. False. If the equation is not kept in balance every step of the way, like any equation, it will not balance at the end.

29. False. Accounting is not always precise; often estimates must be used. See question 30.

30. True.

A few words from you ...

31.

	ASSETS	LIABILITIES	EQUITY
INCREASE	debit	credit	credit
DECREASE	credit	debit	debit
USUAL BALANCE	debit	credit	credit

36. Analysis:

	Accounts	A, L, or E?	+ or -	Amount
1)	cash	A	-	$500
	motor	A	+	4500
	note payable	L	+	4000
2)	supplies on hand	A	+	850
	accounts payable	L	+	850
3)	cash	A	+	1000
	contributed capital	E	+	1000
4)	cash	A	-	200
	prepaid advertising	A	+	200
5)	cash	A	+	500
	accounts receivable	A	-	500

Entries:

1) Motor   4500
        Cash   500
        Note payable   4000

2) Supplies on hand   850
        Accounts payable   850

3) Cash   1000
        Contributed capital   1000

4) Prepaid advertising   200
        Cash   200

5) Cash   500
        Accounts receivable   500

T-accounts:

cash			
beg.	600	500	(1)
(3)	1000	200	(4)
(5)	500		
end	1400		

accounts receivable			
beg.	500	500	(5)

prepaid advertising		
(4)	200	
end	200	

supplies on hand	
beg.	80
(2)	850
end	930

launch, net	
beg.	4000

computer, net	
beg.	4000

motor, net	
(1)	4500

accounts payable		
	850	(2)

note payable		
	4000	(1)

contributed capital		
	7000	beg.
	1000	(3)
	8000	end

retained earnings		
	2180	beg.

Odyssey, Inc.
Balance Sheet
at April 30, 1995

ASSETS

Cash	$1,400	
Prepaid advertising	200	
Supplies on hand	930	
Launch, net	4,000	
Computer, net	4,000	
Motor, net	4,500	
Total assets		**$15,030**

LIABILITIES

Accounts payable	$850	
Note payable	4,000	4,850

OWNERS' EQUITY

Contributed capital	8,000	
Retained earnings	2,180	10,180
Total liabilities & equity		**$15,030**

● And just for the fun of it:

The double entry system is just over 500 years old. Rules have changed with industrial progress, but the basic methods have not. Fra Luca Paciolo, in 1494, published his "Summa de Arithmetica, Geometria, Proportioni et Proportionalita." He was said to be the teacher to the sons of the merchants of Venice who were destined to inherit their fathers' profitable businesses. Later, James Peele is credited with the development of the journal entry system.

CHAPTER 3

INCOME MEASUREMENT AND OPERATING DECISIONS

... to earn a little and to spend a little less, ...
Robert Louis Stevenson

OVERVIEW

In Chapter 2, we discussed the fundamental accounting model and transaction analysis. Journal entries and T-accounts were used to record the results of transaction analysis for investing and financing decisions that affect balance sheet accounts. In this chapter, we continue our detailed look at financial statements, particularly the income statement. The purpose of this chapter is to build on your knowledge by discussing concepts for the measurement of revenues and expenses and by illustrating transaction analysis for operating decisions.

LEARNING OBJECTIVES

1. Understand the time period assumption and the elements of the income statement.

2. Explain a typical business operating cycle.

3. Explain the cash basis and accrual basis of accounting.

4. Apply the revenue, matching, and cost principles to determine the timing and amount of revenue and expense recognition.

5. Explain the phases in the accounting cycle and how the differences between the operating cycle and accounting cycle affect the income measurement process.

6. Apply transaction analysis to analyze and record the effects of operating activities on the financial statements.

7. Prepare a simple income statement.

CHAPTER OUTLINE

What is the time-period assumption?

The results of an entity's operations are reported for **short periods**, for example, a quarter, or a year

- entity may exist for a very long period, but information is needed at frequent intervals
- public corporations required by SEC to report quarterly, in addition to annually
- year end need not conform to calendar
    - ◊may be specifically defined as a certain date
    - ◊may conform to entity's natural business cycle

What are the elements of the income statement?

Revenues are inflows of assets

- result from ongoing operations of entity
- increase assets or decrease liabilities

Expenses are outflows of assets

- result from ongoing operations, involving the generation of revenue
- use up assets or increase liabilities

Gains are inflows of assets from non-operating activities

- not related to entity's central business

Losses are asset outflows from activities other than the company's central business

---

Reference point: Now you have learned all the elements of financial statements. Take a few minutes to review Exhibit 1 in your text.

What is an operating cycle?

An **operating cycle** is also known as a cash-to-cash cycle

- the time it takes to purchase goods or services, sell them to customers, and collect cash from customers
- two primary concerns:
    - ◊**timing**: when should revenues and expenses be recorded?
    - ◊**measurement**: what amounts should be recorded?

Reference point: Exhibit 3 in your text illustrates a typical business cycle

What do we mean by *cash* versus *accrual* accounting?

On the **cash basis**, revenues are recorded when cash is collected, and expenses when cash is paid out

       •no attention is paid to when these are earned or incurred

       •this method is not appropriate for external reporting

           ◊no assets or liabilities other than cash are recorded

           ◊income can easily be manipulated

               ·for example, receipts can be postponed until another period, thus decreasing income

On the **accrual basis**, assets, liabilities, revenue and expense are recognized when the transaction that caused them is complete

       •**revenue principle**: revenues are recorded when earned regardless of when cash is received

           ◊company has delivered goods or services

           ◊customer delivers cash, or a promise to pay

           ◊collection is reasonably assured

       •**matching principle**: expenses are recognized when incurred, regardless of when cash is paid

           ◊expenses are matched to the revenues they helped generate

       •**cost principle** (see Chapter 2): revenues (assets to be received from customers) and expenses (assets used up in generating revenues) must be recorded at their cash equivalent value

       •cash flows resulting from revenues and expenses are reported on a separate statement, the Statement of Cash Flows

       •**time line** showing activities, dates, and amounts is useful for organizing data, and determining timing and amounts of transactions

What is an accounting cycle?

The **accounting cycle** is concerned with the accounting period, not necessarily the business operating cycle. The accounting cycle typically involves a number of steps in two phases:

- Phase 1, during the period
  - ◊transaction analysis
    - ·we can use the abbreviations dr and cr (or Dr. and Cr.) to stand for debit and credit, respectively
    - ·we need to add detail to model to incorporate the details of retained earnings: revenues, expenses, dividends
      - ∞dividends are not an expense but do decrease retained earnings, and are thus recorded as a debit (dr) when declared
  - ◊revenue and expense journal entries
    - ·revenues increase retained earnings, so recorded as a Cr. (credit)
    - ·expenses decrease retained earnings, so recorded as a Dr. (debit)
    - ·four basic types of revenue and expense entries
      - ∞cash coincides with recognition
      - ∞promise to pay coincides with recognition
      - ∞**accrual**: revenue earned or expense incurred during accounting period, but cash will be received or paid in a later period
      - ∞**deferral**: cash received or paid during the accounting period, but revenue will not be earned or expense incurred until a later period
  - ◊entries posted to ledger (similar to T-accounts)
- Phase 2, at end of the period
  - ◊trial balance
  - ◊adjusting journal entries
  - ◊financial statements
  - ◊closing entries

What is an unadjusted income statement?

An income statement can be prepared from transactions reflecting operating activities
- it does not contain *adjusting* entries (accruals and deferrals)
- thus, it is called an **unadjusted income statement**
- the same is true of balance sheet until adjustments have been made

51

QUESTIONS AND EXERCISES

Multiple Choice:

Read each question carefully and choose the best of the five answers given. Remember that more than one answer may in some way be *true* , but you are looking for the *best* answer. Circle the letter of the correct answer.

1. The concept that a business may exist for years, even centuries, yet must report its results in shorter time periods to satisfy the needs of decision makers is the

    a. dual aspect assumption

    b. separate entity assumption.

    c. time-period assumption.

    d. continuity assumption.

    e. full disclosure principle.

2. An interim report is a(n)

    a. report issued quarterly, in addition to annual audited statements.

    b. report issued right after year-end, before the auditors have had a chance to look over the books.

    c. annual report.

    d. estimated set of financial statements prepared in lieu of actually closing the books.

    e. news release by management summarizing some recent events.

3. Revenues are defined as

    a. increases in cash.

    b. increases to assets.

    c. decreases in liabilities.

    d. the opposite of expenses.

    e. answers b and/or c above.

4. When an expense occurs, _____ decrease or _____ increase, resulting from the generation of revenues.

    a. liabilities; assets

    b. cash; accounts receivable

    c. cash; accounts payable

    d. assets; liabilities

    e. revenues; liabilities

5. Gains are similar to _____ and losses are similar to _____ .

    a. revenues; expenses

    b. expenses; revenues

    c. debits; credits

    d. credits; debits

    e. assets; liabilities

6. The time it takes a company to purchase goods or services from suppliers, sell them to customers, and collect cash from customers is

    a. one month.

    b. one year.

    c. the operating cycle.

    d. the accounting cycle

    e. either c or d above

7. The _____ basis of accounting recognizes revenues and expenses when the cash changes hands, whereas the _____ basis of accounting recognizes revenues and expenses when the transaction that causes them is complete or nearly so.

    a. proprietorship; corporate

    b. American; international

    c. cash; accrual

    d. conservative; liberal

    e. financial; managerial

8. *When* revenues or expenses should be recognized is a _____ issue; *what amounts* should be recognized is a _____ issue.

    a. primary; secondary

    b. cost-benefit; materiality

    c. matching; full-disclosure

    d. time-period; conservatism

    e. timing; measurement

9. The earnings process is considered complete when

    a. the company has a written purchase order from the customer.

    b. the company has delivered, or substantially delivered, the promised goods or services to the customer.

    c. the company has the goods on hand, or has begun the service promised.

    d. the customer has given the company a deposit on the promised goods or services.

    e. the company has shipped the goods to its warehouse in the customer's town.

10. Under the revenue principle, revenue is recorded as long as the earnings process is substantially complete, there has been payment or a promise to pay, and

    a. the check is in the mail.

    b. the customer is satisfied with the product or service.

    c. collection is reasonably assured.

    d. there is no possibility that the product will be returned.

    e. the sale has been entered into the seller's accounts receivable.

11. Daphne is a crew member at a local McDonald's restaurant. She worked 30 hours *this* week, but will not be paid until *next* Friday. However, McDonald's has recognized her earned wages as an expense for this week, not for next Friday. This is an example of

    a. income manipulation.

    b. the matching principle.

    c. the time-period assumption.

    d. the conservatism principle.

    e. the continuity assumption.

12. Revenues are measured at the cash or cash-equivalent value of the assets received from customers in accordance with the
    a. cash basis.
    b. cost principle.
    c. matching principle.
    d. revenue recognition principle.
    e. unit-of-measure assumption.

13. Revenues _____ retained earnings, and therefore normally have a _____ balance; expenses _____ retained earnings, and thus have a _____ balance.
    a. increase; debit; decrease; credit
    b. increase; credit; decrease; debit
    c. decrease; debit; increase; credit
    d. decrease; credit; increase; debit
    e. increase; credit; decrease; credit

14. An accrual occurs when cash will be received or paid _____ revenues or expenses are recognized. a deferral occurs when cash is received or paid _____ revenues or expenses are recognized.
    a. at the same time; before
    b. at the same time; after
    c. before; after
    d. after; before
    e. before; at the same time

For the next five questions we will return to the McDonald's example used in Chapter 2 of this Study Guide and use some typical income-related transactions that might occur for this restaurant chain.

15. A customer purchases three sundaes at a neighborhood McDonald's, paying $2.07. To record the sale the restaurant would be likely to first debit _____ and credit _____. The entry to record the cost of the items sold would then credit _____.

    a. sales; cash; cost of goods sold

    b. cash; sales; inventory

    c. accounts receivable; sales; inventory

    d. sales; accounts receivable; cost of goods sold

    e. sales; cash; accounts payable

16. The company's home office receives reports from franchisees for a certain period showing that revenues due the home office totaled 40 million dollars. This amount will be collected by McDonald's within 30 days. The home office entry to record this revenue would involve a debit to _____ and a credit to _____ .

    a. cash; accounts receivable

    b. accounts receivable; cash

    c. cash; revenue from franchisees

    d. accounts receivable; revenue from franchisees

    e. accounts receivable; deferred income

17. A local artist is paid $300 to paint holiday pictures on the windows of a restaurant. The remaining portion of the artist's fee, another $250, will be paid to the artist in 30 days. The artist's work is completed and billed. The correct entry for the store to record this transaction is

a. Miscellaneous store expense	550	
Cash		300
Accounts payable		250
b. Miscellaneous store expense	300	
Cash		300
c. Miscellaneous store expense	300	
Deferred expense	250	
Cash		300
Accounts payable		250
d. Miscellaneous store expense	550	
Cash		550
e. Miscellaneous store expense	300	
Cash		300
Accounts payable		250

18. A franchisee pays a local appliance repair service $400 to calibrate the thermostats on all the ovens in the store after they were found to be erratic in their performance. The entry to record this transaction would be

a. Equipment	400	
Accounts payable		400
b. Equipment	400	
Cash		400
c. Repair expense	400	
Cash		400
d. Repair expense	400	
Accounts payable		400
e. Wages expense	400	
Cash		400

19. McDonald's purchased insurance for $5000 cash to cover product liability for the coming year, beginning the first of next month. The entry to record this purchase would be

a. Insurance expense	5000	
Cash		5000
b. Prepaid insurance	5000	
Cash		5000
c. Cash	5000	
Prepaid insurance		5000
d. Cash	5000	
Insurance expense		5000
e. Accounts receivable	5000	
Cash		5000

20. An income statement prepared to reflect operating activities, before revenue and expense accounts are brought up to date by adjusting entries, is called an unadjusted statement because

      a. it still contains a lot of mistakes.

      b. the total debits do not necessarily equal the total credits.

      c. it does not reflect generally accepted accounting principles based on accrual accounting.

      d. the balance sheet has not yet been prepared.

      e. dividends have not been taken into account.

True or False?

In the space in front of each of the following statements, place the letter "T" or "F" to indicate whether you think the statement is true or false. Remember, if you think a statement is false, try to reword it to make it true. This will help to reinforce your understanding of the concepts involved.

_____ 21. Generally accepted accounting principles require a company to report results for each year, ending on December 31.

_____ 22. Peripheral operations are those not related to the central business of the company. Gains and losses from these are reported separately in the income statement.

_____ 23. A company can only receive cash from a customer after it has completed delivery of a product or service to that customer.

_____ 24. A company may choose either the cash or the accrual basis of accounting for public reporting purposes.

_____ 25. In terms of revenue recognition, a customer's promise to pay is considered as good as the receipt of cash.

_____ 26. For most (not necessarily all) businesses, the conditions for revenue recognition are met at the point of delivery of goods or services.

_____ 27. If an auditor should disagree with a client over a question of revenue recognition, the auditor must ultimately defer to the client, since the client is paying the auditor for his or her services.

_____ 28. The accounting cycle is virtually the same for all companies, but the business cycle is not.

_____ 29. When an employee has earned wages in a one accounting period and will be paid in the next period, an adjusting entry will be necessary.

_____ 30. Adjusting entries affect only income statement, and not balance sheet, accounts.

A Few Words from You ...

Answer each of the following with a paragraph or two, or appropriate entries or calculations.

31. **What are the rules of debit and credit for stockholders' equity?** Fill in the following detailed stockholders' equity table with the correct abbreviation—Dr or Cr—to indicate the proper treatment of each element of stockholders' equity.

		STOCKHOLDERS	EQUITY	
	PAID IN CAPITAL	RETAINED	EARNINGS	
	-	DIVIDENDS	REVENUES	EXPENSES
INCREASE				
DECREASE				
NORMAL BALANCE				

The general rule (explained in Chapter 2) for debits and credits indicates that stockholders' equity is increased by a credit and decreased by a debit. Why, then, do the individual elements of stockholders' equity in the table above not appear to follow this rule?

32. **How does a manufacturer account for wages?** In your textbook, it was explained that in keeping with the matching principle, an employee's wages are expensed in the period in which they are earned and in which the employee generates revenues for the company regardless of when the employee is actually paid. As an example, we looked at the wages of workers in a service company. How do you suppose the wages of a factory worker, who is building a product that the company will later sell, are expensed? When do these wages become an expense? What are they called until that time? Explain your answer.

33. **How long is an operating cycle?** Can you think of any companies or industries in which the operating cycle may be exceptionally long—perhaps more than a year? Is there a limit on the length of an operating cycle? How would you imagine these companies might recognize revenue? How would they apply the matching principle to recognize expenses?

34. **Where can you buy a hamburger?** The following extract from the McDonald's 1992 Annual Report shows revenues by geographic segment for 1990, 1991, and 1992.

($ millions)

	1992	1991	1990
United States	$ 3749.4	$ 3710.2	$ 3871.0
Europe / Africa	2187.0	1806.0	1635.8
Canada	595.1	629.5	650.7
Pacific	434.6	392.5	339.9
Latin America	167.2	156.8	142.2
Total revenues	$ 7133.3	$ 6695.0	$ 6639.6

Which geographic segment shows the greatest contribution to total revenues?
Which segment shows the most growth?
Why might this information be important to the company? to an investor?
Why might this information be important to someone with an interest in Sbarro (the company used as the chapter example in your text)?

Team up!

These projects are meant to be done in teams of 4 or 5 members, unless otherwise noted. Pool your knowledge and abilities to find the best answers!

35. **When are franchise fees earned?** In the prospectus accompanying its initial public offering of stock, a certain company noted that franchise fees are recorded as revenue upon execution of the franchise sales agreement. After an initial down payment, which is not required in all cases, collections of fees are generally made after the franchise unit is actually delivered. Does this method of revenue recognition meet all the criteria you learned? Explain.

A condensed version of the income statement of this company is given below. Assume your team is going to pool funds to make a substantial investment in this company. What questions about their methods of recognizing franchise fee revenue would you want answered before you would be willing to accept the numbers on their income statement? Is franchise fee revenue a critical figure?

Revenues:	
Net sales	$3,601,362
Initial franchise fees	9,081,500
Rent and monthly franchise fees	489,991
Other income	156,738
	13,329,591
Costs and expenses:	
Product costs	3,031,060
Operating	3,474,985
Selling, general, administrative	2,482,693
Depreciation, amortization	204,080
Interest and financing	94,463
	9,287,281
Earnings before taxes	4,042,310
Taxes on income	2,148,000
Net earnings	$1,894,310

36. **Lisa and Charley get down to business.** Let us now return to Odyssey, Inc., the small business for which you developed a balance sheet in Chapter 2 (see Chapter 2, question 36). Assume the boating season is now underway, and during the first couple of weeks, they have the following transactions:

a. They remove the winter cover from a yacht, air and clean the boat, and perform other small maintenance to prepare it for the season. They leave the owner a bill for $100.

b. The owner of another yacht contracts with them to paint his boat, for $1,000. He gives them an advance of $200. The remainder will be paid when they complete the job. They estimate that they will do this at the end of next week, and it will take them two days.

c. At the marina they purchase $10 of gasoline for their launch, plus $50 of supplies that they use immediately to refinish the teak on another boat, adding these amounts to their account at the marina.

d. The owner of the boat in (c) above pays them $150 for helping him refinish the teak on his boat.

e. They purchase $200 of paint for the boat in (b) above on account.

FIRST, pair off and analyze each transaction, using the model in your textbook:

       Accounts   A, L, or E?   + or -   Amount

(a)

(b)

(c)

(d)

(e)

SECOND, join with another pair. Compare analyses. Do you agree? Resolve any disagreement by discussing the issues involved, and decide on a correct analysis. Remember that the names of accounts do not have to be precisely the same if they convey virtually the same meaning. Prepare a journal entry for each transaction, and post your journal entries to T-accounts. T-accounts from the concluding balance sheet in Chapter 2, question 36, are provided as a starting point.

Entries:

(a)

(b)

(c)

(d)

(e)

T-accounts:

Cash	Accounts receivable	Prepaid advertising
beg. 1400		beg. 200

Supplies on hand	Launch, net	Computer, net
beg. 930	beg. 4000	beg. 4000

Motor, net	Accounts payable	Note payable
beg. 4500	850 beg.	4000 beg.

Contributed capital	Retained earnings	Revenues
8000 beg.	2180 beg.	

Operating expense	Launch expense	Deferred income

FINALLY, as in the previous chapter, combine two groups of four, and compare your T-accounts. Do you agree? Resolve any disagreements, then make up a simple income statement for these few days' transactions.

Odyssey, Inc.
Income Statement
for the week ended May 6, 1995

37. **What if Odyssey were a cash basis company?** Look over the income statement you prepared for Odyssey, Inc. in question 36. How do you think this income statement would look if it had been prepared on a cash basis? Prepare a cash-basis income statement for Odyssey, Inc. Which statement is a better indicator or the period's results? Why?

38. **Make up your own questions.** Your textbook contains financial statements for Toys "R" Us in the appendix just before the index. Make up five revenue and expense transactions that this company might typically encounter. Now, exchange transactions with another group. Prepare journal entries for the other group's transactions. As a class, compare the transactions that groups thought of. How many different types of revenue or expense transactions were there? Do you think your class thought of all the types of entries that this company might have? Explain.

39. **What makes an accounting "system" necessary?** Have one member of your team carry a small note pad with them for one day and write down every event that happens that has an economic effect on them: any pay they receive; a gift; a loan; every purchase; anything they are given or give to someone else in other than cash; repayment of a loan.

After this is done, get together and try to make sense of this list. How can you go about organizing it? Are there categories you could break the items into? How would you go about summarizing this team member's "economic day?"

Do you see that you are designing an accounting and reporting system for this person? Compare and contrast it to what you would expect to find for a business.

And just for the fun of it ...

This simple crossword puzzle reviews vocabulary from Chapters 2 and 3 (and perhaps a word or two from Chapter 1). How much of it can you solve without checking back to the chapters? The end-of-chapter "key terms" lists are a good reference if you need help.

Across

1. By retained earnings, we mean those earnings that are _____ in the business, not distributed to owners.
3. A liability is increased with a ____.
5. The _____ principle requires that assets be recorded at the cash paid plus the cash equivalent value of other assets given to acquire the assets.
7. Item with future benefit to the entity.
8. Abbreviation for a company whose owners are legally separate from the business.
11. Accounting method that requires revenues to be recorded when they are earned.
14. General Accounting Office.
15. Credit.
16. The cycle from the purchase of goods for resale through the collection of accounts from customers.
17. The assumption that divides the life of an entity into shorter periods for reporting.
19. A visual representation of a series of business activities over time.
23. Original entry to record a transaction.
25. A liability arises out of a _____ transaction.
27. Accounting information is measured and reported in the national monetary _____ where the entity is headquartered.
28. Many businesses choose a year-end to _____ their natural business cycle.
29. The ____ principle requires that expenses be recorded in the period in which they were incurred in earning revenue.
30. Liability.
34. The assumption that a business will operate into the foreseeable future.
35. A _____ account is a simplified representation of a ledger page.

69

Down:

2. An exchange between a business and an external party.
3. _____ basis accounting records expenses when they are paid for.
4. Debit.
5. Often the last word in an entity's name.
6. Business transactions are kept ___ from those of the owners for accounting purposes.
9. Chief Financial Officer.
10. A company issues shares of stock to the public to _____ capital to expand the business.
12. Inflows of assets into an entity.
13. Certified Public Accountant.
14. Increases to equity from peripheral activities.
18. Increase to an asset.
20. For _____ businesses, revenue is earned when goods or services are delivered.
21. Decrease in equity from peripheral activities.
22. Financial Accounting Standard.
24. Debits are shown on the _____ side of T-accounts.
26. A standard format to accumulate changes to a financial statement item.
31. It is customary in recording a journal entry to first enter the debit(s), then to record the account(s) credited _____ the debit(s).
32. Accrual accounting recognizes expenses when they are earned, not when they are _____.
33. Certified Internal Auditor.

SOLUTIONS

Multiple Choice:

1. (c) 2. (a) 3. (e) 4. (d) 5. (a) 6. (c) 7. (c) 8. (e) 9. (b) 10. (c) 11. (b) 12. (b) 13. (b) 14. (d) 15. (b) 16. (d) 17. (a) 18. (c) 19. (b) 20. (c)

True or False:

21. False. A company need not choose December 31 as their year-end. Any date at all may be chosen, as long as it is used consistently.

22. True.

23. False. The delivery of goods and services and the receipt of cash need not, and often do not, occur at the same time.

24. False. For external reporting, the accrual basis is required by GAAP.

25. True.

26. True.

27. False. The fact that the client pays the auditor does not excuse the auditor from the professional responsibility to ensure that results are reported in conformance with generally accepted accounting practices.

28. True.

29. True.

30. False. Adjusting entries are made to both income statement and balance sheet accounts.

A Few Words from You ...

31.

		STOCKHOLDERS	EQUITY	
	PAID IN CAPITAL	RETAINED	EARNINGS	
	-	DIVIDENDS	REVENUES	EXPENSES
INCREASE	Cr	Dr	Cr	Dr
DECREASE	Dr	Cr	Dr	Cr
NORMAL BALANCE	Cr	Dr	Cr	Dr

Team up!

36. Analysis:

Accounts	A, L, or E?	+ or −	Amount
(a) Accounts receivable	A	+	100
Revenues	E	+	100
(b) Cash	A	+	200
Deferred revenue	L	+	200
(c) Launch expense	E	−	10
Supplies expense	E	−	50
Accounts payable	L	+	60
(d) Cash	A	+	150
Revenues	E	+	150
(e) Supplies on hand	A	+	200
Accounts payable	L	+	200

Entries:

(a)	Accounts receivable	100	
	Revenues		100
(b)	Cash	200	
	Deferred income		200
(c)	Launch expense	10	
	Operating expense	50	
	Accounts payable		60
(d)	Cash	150	
	Revenues		150
(e)	Supplies on hand	200	
	Accounts payable		200

T-accounts:

Cash	
beg. 1400	
(b) 200	
(d) 150	

Accounts receivable	
(a) 100	

Prepaid advertising	
beg. 200	

Supplies on hand	
beg. 930	
(e) 200	

Launch, net	
beg. 4000	

Computer, net	
beg. 4000	

Motor, net	
beg. 4500	

Accounts payable	
	850 beg.
	60 (c)
	200 (e)

Note payable	
	4000 beg.

Contributed capital	
	8000 beg.

Retained earnings	
	2180 beg.

Revenues	
	100 (a)
	150 (d)

Operating expense	
(c) 50	

Launch expense	
(c) 10	

Deferred income	
	200 (b)

73

Odyssey, Inc.
Income Statement
for the week ended May 6, 1995

Revenues	$250
Operating expenses	50
Launch expense	10
Net income	$190

And just for the fun of it...

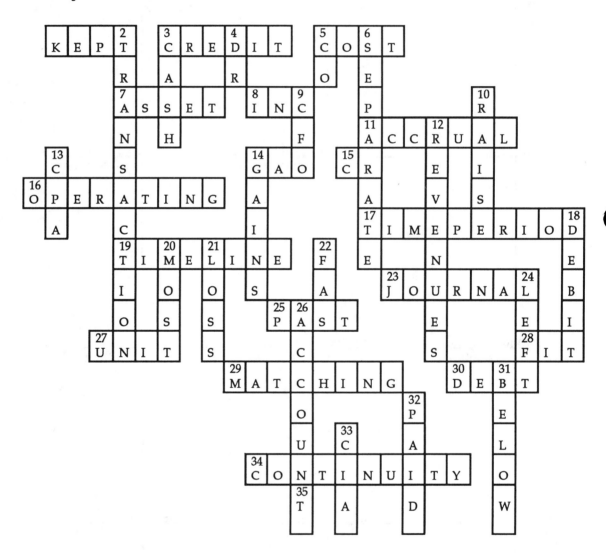

CHAPTER 4

THE ADJUSTMENT PROCESS AND FINANCIAL STATEMENT PREPARATION

I balanced all, brought all to mind ...
William Butler Yeats

OVERVIEW

Chapters 2 and 3 introduced you to the fundamental accounting model and transaction analysis. The chapters also discussed the use of journal entries and T-accounts to record the results of transaction analysis for operating, investing, and financing activities during the accounting period. In this chapter, we will build on your knowledge and discuss the income determination activities at the end of the accounting period: the adjustment process, preparation of financial statements, and the closing process. For those wanting information on formal record keeping procedures in the accounting cycle, supplements to the chapter are included.

LEARNING OBJECTIVES

1. Explain the purpose of a trial balance and construct one from T-account balances.

2. Analyze deferrals and accruals at the end of the period and prepare necessary adjustments to update accounts for proper matching of revenues and expenses.

3. Prepare a complete set of financial statements: income statement, statement of stockholders' equity, balance sheet, and statement of cash flows.

4. Explain the closing process and prepare closing entries.

5. (Supplement A) Utilize a formal general journal and a general ledger format in preparing journal entries and accumulating account balances.

6. (Supplement B) Construct a year-end worksheet which includes a trial balance, adjustments, and amounts for the income statement and balance sheet.

7. (Supplement C) Explain and prepare reversing entries.

CHAPTER OUTLINE

Why are adjusting entries necessary?

The operating and accounting cycles do not necessarily end at the same point

Some internal activities do not result in an exchange with an outside party but do have to be recorded

- •knowledge and judgment required rather than supporting documents
- •accruals: revenues earned, or expenses incurred, before cash changes hands
- •deferrals: receipts or payments of cash or other assets in advance of the related revenue or expense recognition

What is a trial balance?

Trial balance is a list of individual accounts in financial statement order, with their ending debit or credit balance

- •unadjusted trial balance done before adjusting entries
- •for internal analysis, not for outside users
- •long lived asset accounts at their historical cost
    - ◊*contra asset* account used for each long-lived asset to record the amount of the asset used up by the date of the trial balance
        - ·contra asset always appears immediately after related asset account
        - ·contra asset, or offset, for equipment is called *accumulated depreciation*
    - ◊asset less contra asset is called net book value or carrying value

How are adjustments done?

Deferrals result from a transaction already recorded

- •analyze original entry
- •determine the correct balances of the accounts at the end of the period
- •record entries to adjust—correct—the accounts

◊original entry may record asset; adjustment records expiration of that asset (decrease an asset, increase expense)

◊original entry may record expense; adjustment moves expense that has not been incurred into an asset account (increase asset, decrease expense)

◊original entry may record unearned revenue; adjustment records amount of that revenue earned as of end of period (decrease liability, increase revenue)

◊original entry may record revenue; adjustment removes unearned portion from revenue and places it in a liability account (decrease revenue, increase liability

Accruals occur when company has earned revenue or incurred expense but no external transaction has occurred

•professional analysis and/or judgment required to determine those activities which should be recorded

◊accrue expenses incurred before cash is paid

◊accrue revenues earned before cash is received

◊expenses and liabilities, or revenues and assets, are increased

Reference point: Carefully review the illustration of adjusting entries for Sbarro, Inc. in your text. Adjustments are a source of confusion to beginning accounting students, so do not be discouraged if these entries do not immediately make sense to you. The only way to thoroughly understand them is through repeated exposure and practice.

How are financial statements prepared?

Financial statements interlock:

•*income statement* : (revenues + gains) - (expenses + losses) = net income

◊**earnings per share (EPS)** also calculated: net income + average shares outstanding for the period

•*statement of retained earnings* : net income + beginning *retained earnings* - dividends = ending *retained earnings*

◊net income comes from the income statement

•*balance sheet* : assets = liabilities + stockholders' equity (contributed capital + retained earnings)

◊retained earnings comes from the statement of retained earnings

statement of cash flows concentrates solely on the items that have caused the balance of the cash account to change

◊classified as operating, investing, and financing activities

◊using cash balance from balance sheet

Reference point: Review Exhibit 4-4 in your text to be sure you understand how the accounts studied to date relate to one another and how they are recorded.

What does does the closing process involve?

Distinction is made between permanent (real) accounts and temporary (nominal) accounts

•**permanent** accounts are balance sheet accounts and are never closed

◊accounts are updated continuously during period

◊ending balance of one period becomes beginning balance of the next

•**temporary** accounts are income statement accounts

◊accounts accumulate data for the current accounting period only

◊balances are transferred to retained earnings at the end of each period, using **closing entries**

·debit accounts with a credit balance for entire amount of balance

·credit accounts with a debit balance for entire amount of balance

·other half of entry is either made to **Income Summary**, a special temporary account used only for closing, or directly to retained earnings

·leaves income statement accounts with zero balances, ready for next period

·generally done only at the end of fiscal year

Final step in cycle is post-closing trial balance, to ensure that debits equal credits and that all temporary accounts are closed

SUPPLEMENT A
THE FORMAL RECORDKEEPING SYSTEM

What are the principal books of account used?

The **general journal** is the book of original entry, where transactions are recorded in chronological order

•entry contains date, accounts debited and credited, and an explanation in enough detail so that the entry can be traced to its source documents

◊this is known as a **audit trail**

The **general ledger,** or the book of final entry, contains information on each individual account in the entity's accounting system

•transfer from the journal to the ledger is known as *posting*

•journal entries and ledger accounts are cross referenced

SUPPLEMENT B
ACCOUNTING WORKSHEETS

How is a worksheet prepared?

Worksheet usually records unadjusted trial balance, adjustments, adjusted trial balance and information for financial statements, including income statement, statement of retained earnings and balance sheet

•set up column headings

•enter unadjusted trial balance from ledger

◊check to see that total of debit column equals total of credit column

•develop and enter adjustments

◊check column balances to be sure they are equal

•complete adjusted trial balance columns by adding adjustments to original accounts in unadjusted trial balance, carrying across original balances of accounts not affected by adjustments

◊again, be sure to check that debits remain equal to credits

•amount for each line in adjusted trial balance is entered in the correct (debit or credit) column under the appropriate financial statement

•income statement columns are added; the difference between them is net income (credit balance) or net loss (debit balance)

◊income tax adjustment is calculated by multiplying this difference by tax rate, and entering adjustment at bottom of worksheet

◊net income is balancing debit in income statement column and credit in the retained earnings column

•retained earnings columns are summed; difference is ending retained earnings, entered as a balancing debit in retained earnings column and as a credit on the balance sheet

◊after retained earnings is entered, the two balance sheet columns should be equal

SUPPLEMENT C
REVERSING ENTRIES

Why are reversing entries needed?

Reversing entries are optional entries at the beginning of a period that reverse, or cancel out, certain adjustments made at the end of the previous period, in order to facilitate routine entries to follow

> •allow routine recording of events, so adjustments are only necessary at end of period
>
> •all accruals can be reversed
>
> •deferrals that created or increased an asset or liability are reversed

QUESTIONS AND EXERCISES

Multiple Choice:

Consider each of the answers to the following questions carefully. More than one may be a *possible* answer. Only one is the *best* answer. Circle the letter of the best answer.

1. Which of the following is an accurate statement about a trial balance?
   a. It assures that the correct accounts have been debited and credited.
   b. It assures that total debits equal total credits.
   c. It assures that accounts were correctly posted from the journal to the ledger.
   d. It assures that all accounts have been updated.
   e. It assures that journal entries were prepared correctly.

2. A contra asset is
   a. really a liability, not an asset.
   b. an incorrectly entered asset.
   c. an offset to an asset account, having a credit balance.
   d. an account used to close an asset.
   e. the opposite of an asset.

3. The net book value, or carrying value, of a long-lived asset
   a. is not meant to represent its market value.
   b. is equal to the value of the asset not yet used up by its owner.
   c. represents the end result of an effort to allocate cost over the life of an asset.
   d. is usually shown on the balance sheet combined with other assets of its kind.
   e. all of the above.

4. An example of a deferral would be
   a. a one-year insurance policy paid for in cash on its effective date.
   b. interest on a loan which is not due to be paid in cash for 6 months.
   c. merchandise sold on account.
   d. merchandise purchased on account.
   e. wages earned but not yet paid.

5. An example of an accrual would be
    a. rent collected from a tenant covering the coming six months.
    b. merchandise sold on account.
    c. merchandise purchased on account.
    d. interest on a loan which is not due to be paid in cash for 6 months.
    e. payment for a one-year subscription to a magazine.

The following list contains balance sheet effects of transactions. Choose the one that fits each situation given in questions 6 – 10, and write the correct letter in the space in front of each question.
    a. increase assets, increase liabilities
    b. increase assets, decrease liabilities
    c. decrease assets, decrease liabilities
    d. decrease assets, increase liabilities
    e. increase assets, increase equity
    f. increase assets, decrease equity
    g. increase liabilities, increase equity
    h. increase liabilities, decrease equity
    i. decrease liabilities, increase equity
    j. decrease liabilities, decrease equity
    k. none of the above

_____ 6. A furniture store receives $200 from a customer as a down payment on a set of furniture to be delivered in a week. Recording this transaction would

_____ 7. An employer records the proper entry to account for 16 hours worked by an employee for which the employee will not be paid until next week. That entry would

_____ 8. The company's purchasing department pays $40 to a publisher for a two-year subscription to a trade journal to begin in two months. The entry to record the payment would

_____ 9. A company records 3 months' interest on a loan the company made to an officer, which will be paid back in one lump sum in two years. The entry to recognize that interest would

82

_____ 10. A lawyer makes a year-end adjustment to account for the expired portion of a retainer fee paid to her six months ago by a client. That adjustment would

11. A company purchased a truck five years ago for $24,000. They have recorded a total of $15,000 of depreciation expense up to this time. The *credit* portion of the entries to record this $15,000 over the years is contained in an account called
    a. trucks.
    b. truck expense.
    c. accumulated depreciation, trucks.
    d. retained earnings.
    e. net book value.

12. Refer to the information in question (11). The difference ($9,000) between the cost of the truck ($24,000) and the $15,000, is the _____ of the truck.
    a. market value
    b. net book value
    c. current cost
    d. selling price
    e. salvage value

13. Auditors allocate more testing time to adjusting entries because
    a. they are more interesting than other entries.
    b. it takes less time to examine them.
    c. they are more prone to errors than other entries.
    d. they have a clearer audit trail.
    e. they were the most recent entries done by the company.

14. Closing entries are made to
    a. assets.
    b. liabilities.
    c. revenue and expense accounts.
    d. all stockholders' equity accounts.
    e. all of the above.

The following questions (15–20) pertain to the appendices to the chapter. If your instructor has not assigned these appendices, you may skip these questions.

15. The general journal links the events of each transaction physically and records them
    a. on separate pages, by account.
    b. chronologically.
    c. monthly.
    d. alphabetically
    e. in classifications, as assets, liabilities, and equity.

16. The process of transferring data from the journal to the ledger is known as
    a. posting.
    b. recording.
    c. copying.
    d. auditing.
    e. processing.

17. Entries made at the start of an accounting period, which are the opposite of certain adjusting entries, are called
    a. contra accounts.
    b. opening entries.
    c. closing entries.
    d. reversing entries
    e. correcting entries.

18. Adjusting entries that can be reversed include
    a. all adjustments related to accruals.
    b. all entries related to deferrals.
    c. deferrals limited to those that created or increased an asset or liability.
    d. only accruals made to existing assets.
    e. both (a) and (c).

19. The primary reason to make reversing entries is that
   a. they make the opening books of account neater.
   b. the adjustments they reverse were never meant to be real entries.
   c. they facilitate the recording of routine transactions during the accounting cycle.
   d. the accounts would be incorrect if they were not done.
   e. they are required by generally accepted accounting principles.

20. An explanation is usually included for every general journal entry because
   a. otherwise the entries would be incomprehensible.
   b. source documents can be destroyed once the entry is made to reduce paper storage.
   c. it provides an audit trail for future reference to the source of the entry.
   d. it ensures that employees do the entries carefully.
   e. it is customary.

True or False?

In the space before each statement, place the letter "T" or "F" to indicate whether the statement is true or false. Check your understanding by rewording each false statement to make it true.

_____ 21. The difference between an accrual adjusting entry and a deferral adjusting entry is in the timing of the cash payment or receipt that gives rise to that entry.

_____ 22. A trial balance is prepared to give an accountant assurance that all the work done up to the point of adjusting entries was done correctly.

_____ 23. The cost of a long-lived asset less the accumulated depreciation on that asset is the net market value of the asset.

_____ 24. The net book value, or carrying value, of an asset does not represent the current market value of the asset.

_____ 25. When a payment is made before an expense is recognized, the asset recorded is known as a deferral.

_____ 26. An accrual results when a company earns revenue after cash has been exchanged.

_____ 27. Since adjusting entries involve estimates, and often judgment on the part of the preparer, they can give rise to "income manipulation."

_____ 28. The flow of information from one statement to the next dictates that the balance sheet should be the first statement prepared.

_____ 29. Temporary or nominal accounts are those used to accumulate data from the current accounting period only.

_____ 30. Closing entries are done to clear income statement accounts to a zero balance and transfer their balances to retained earnings.

The following questions should only be answered if you have been assigned the appendices to the chapter.

_____ 31. The general journal and general ledger are only used by those companies who still maintain handwritten books of account.

_____ 32. The general journal is kept by account; the general ledger is chronological.

_____ 33. A year-end worksheet is an optional working paper that is used to provide data needed to construct adjusting journal entries and prepare financial statements.

_____ 34. Reversing entries are done to facilitate routine entries while still properly allocating revenues and expenses between periods.

_____ 35. All adjusting entries can be reversed on the first day of the new accounting period.

● A Few Words from You ...

Answer each question in this section with calculations or entries, or a short paragraph, as indicated.

36. **Why do we keep two accounts for long-lived assets?** Explain why it might be useful to you, an outsider—whether an investor, or a creditor, or an analyst—to know both the original cost and the accumulated depreciation on a long-lived asset.

37. **When is something an adjustment and when is it a routine transaction?** Explain the difference between accrued revenues and accounts receivable. Explain the difference between accrued expenses and accounts payable.

38. **What happens when adjustments are forgotten?** The following chart shows a number of "errors of omission" that a company might make. All are instances of overlooked adjusting entries. For each one, first complete the "current year" columns. Write "O" if the effect of the error would be an overstatement of that financial statement element, that is, the item would be too large. Write "U" if that item would be understated, that is, too small, and "N" if there would be no effect on that item, or if that item would be correct. After you complete the "current year" columns, assume that the company continues into a new year, and no one discovers the error. No adjustment or correction is

made, so no reversing entries are made either. In the new year, routine entries are done as usual. What would be the effect on the new year of the *prior year's* uncorrected errors? Complete the chart for the "following year." For each year indicate the effect on assets (A), liabilities (L), equity (E), net income (I) and retained earnings (R).

	current year					following year				
	A	L	E	I	R	A	L	E	I	R
The entry to record depreciation on an asset is not recorded in the current year										
A one-year retainer fee was booked as a liability at the beginning of the year. It has expired, but no entry was made.										
A two-year insurance policy was recorded as an asset 6 months ago. No further entries have been made.										
The entry to record wages earned this period to be paid at the beginning of next period is omitted.										
The entry to record interest on a note receivable, earned but not due for two months, was omitted.										

Can you make any general observations, based on your answers, on the effect of errors in accruals on net income and retained earnings?

39. **Why are revenues and expenses not accumulated?** Explain in your own words why revenue, expense and dividend accounts—so-called "temporary" accounts—accumulate data for only one period, then are zeroed out to retained earnings, while balance sheet accounts—so-called "permanent" accounts—accumulate data continuously and are never closed. Why not do the same thing—either accumulate data continuously, or close every period—to all accounts?

40. **Is there another way to do this?** Your textbook gives more than one option for recording the original entries for deferrals, and the material in the appendices to the chapter shows that there is more than one way to develop and record adjustments. Can you think of and describe another device companies might use for recording adjustments that would serve the purpose of facilitating routine entries, and eliminate the need for reversals?

Team up!

These assignments are meant to be done in teams of about four people, so that you can assist one another in preparing the best solutions.

41. **What items need to be adjusted?** One way of thinking of adjustments is to see them in four groups of items:
1. Expense now, cash paid later.
2. Revenues now, cash received later.
3. Cash paid now, expense later.
4. Cash received now, revenue later.

Try to think of two or three examples of each one of these. It might help you to first imagine a specific company, so that you can deal with realistic situations. What about American Airlines (AMR Corp.)? Wendy's? Carnival Cruise Lines? What adjustments might they need to make at year-end?

42. **The Odyssey continues ...** Lisa and Charley have continued their business throughout the Summer. It is the end of the New England boating season, and most owners who have not already secured their boats for the winter are preparing to do so. Lisa and Charley want to sail south to continue their business in a warmer climate during the winter. They have to leave before the hurricane season makes the trip unwise. They have the following trial balance for their final (partial) month of business, and want to prepare financial statements before sailing at the end of the week, so they will know how they did for the summer.

Cash	$7,000	
Accounts receivable	500	
Supplies on hand	200	
Prepaid insurance	1,200	
Computer	5,000	
Accumulated depreciation, computer	2,000	
Launch	4,000	
Accumulated depreciation, launch		$1,000
Motor	4,500	
Accumulated depreciation, motor		
Accounts payable		200
Deferred income		2,500
Paid in capital		8,000
Retained earnings		7,380
Revenues		3,650
Operating expense	900	
Wages expense		1,200
Miscellaneous expense	230	
	$25,530	$23,930

a. Review the trial balance above, as a group. Do you find any errors? Can you see what they are? Correct them now.

b. Next, review the trial balance and identify the accounts that in your judgment would be likely to need adjusting entries. At this point, if you are covering Supplement B to the chapter (on the accounting worksheet), prepare a worksheet for Odyssey and put your trial balance on it, including the corrections you made in part (a). If you are not using worksheets in your class, simply make the corrections to the trial balance above. Now, prepare adjusting journal entries for Odyssey, Inc. Clearly you have not been given any numbers to use. Use your professional judgment! Decide as a group on numbers that seem *logical* , given the information you have. Make up adjustments using these numbers, either posting them to your worksheet or simply preparing them in general journal form, depending upon which format you are using.

c. Exchange papers with another group. Check the other group's adjustments. Are they logical? Have they missed any, in your judgment? Once you have a set of adjustments that you believe to be complete and correct, use them to prepare financial statements, either completing your worksheet, or on a separate piece of paper. Prepare only an income statement, a statement of retained earnings, and a balance sheet.

d. Now exchange papers back again, this time including your newly-prepared financial statements. Check the statements that were made, including the adjustments you made up. Do you think they are correct? Do you agree with any changes that were made to your adjustments? Discuss any of these issues with the other team, and resolve the differences. You are the managers! You'll all learn more in the process. Once you are satisfied with the results, prepare closing entries for Odyssey, Inc. Which accounts will *not* be closed? Why?

Closing entries:

And just for the fun of it ...

The following scrambled words are all vocabulary from this chapter. Use the brief definitions given below the list (in no particular order) to help you unscramble each one.

1. CLARAUC
2. MTJESTDUAN
3. RTDAIUTALI (2 words)
4. KVLETNEAOBOU (3 words)
5. GCOLNIS
6. RATOCN
7. LEERFADR
8. LNJUOAR
9. REDGEL
10. TEMPRANEN
11. PERTRAMOY
12. SERVEGNRI
13. LACELINTBARA (2 words)
14. MACESIRMUMYON (2 words)

CLUES: (not in the order the words appear)

Cash lag.

Debit the credits, credit the debits.

Won't last.

Original entry.

Equality check.

Clues to the source.

Back out.

Opposite.

Correction.

Gather income.

Final entry.

Cash lead.

Not market.

Forever.

SOLUTIONS

Multiple choice:
1. (b) 2. (c) 3. (c) 4. (a) 5. (d) 6. (a) 7. (h) 8. (k) 9. (e) 10. (i) 11. (c) 12. (b) 13. (c) 14. (c) 15. (b) 16. (a) 17. (d) 18. (e) 19. (c) 20. (c)

True or false:
21. True.

22. False. The trial balance actually assures only the equality of debits and credits. Other errors could exist that will not be evident in a simple examination of the trial balance.

23. False. The cost of a long-lived asset less accumulated depreciation is the net book value of the asset. This is not meant to approximate market value, but only measures the remaining usefulness of the asset to the company that owns it.

24. True.

25. True.

26. False. An accrual results when a company has earned revenue *before* receiving cash or another asset..

27. True.

28. False. Since the retained earnings portion of the balance sheet results directly from the addition of the period's net income, it is necessary to first prepare the income statement, and the reconciliation of retained earnings.

29. True.

30. True.

31. False. The general journal and general ledger are used by companies with either handwritten or computerized accounting systems. They may look slightly different, but their basic structure and content are the same.

32. False. The general journal is chronological; the ledger is kept by account.

33. True.

34. True.

35. False. Only accruals, and deferrals that create or increase an asset or liability, are reversed.

38.

	current year					following year				
	A	L	E	I	R	A	L	E	I	R
The entry to record depreciation on an asset is not recorded in the current year	O	N	O	O	O	O	N	O	N	O
A one-year retainer fee was booked as a liability at the beginning of the year. It has expired, but no entry was made.	N	O	U	U	U	N	O	U	N	U
A two year insurance policy was recorded as an asset 6 months ago. No further entries have been made.	O	N	O	O	O	O	N	O	N	O
The entry to record wages earned this period, to be paid at the beginning o next period, is omitted.	N	U	O	O	O	N	N	N	U	N
The entry to record interest on a note receivable, earned but not due for two months, was omitted.	U	N	U	U	U	N	N	N	O	N

Team up:

42.   a. The trial balance does not balance. Accumulated depreciation on the computer should be in the credit column. Wages expense should have a debit balance.

And just for the fun of it:

The words are:

1. ACCRUAL
2. ADJUSTMENT
3. AUDIT TRAIL
4. NET BOOK VALUE
5. CLOSING
6. CONTRA
7. DEFERRAL
8. JOURNAL
9. LEDGER
10. PERMANENT
11. TEMPORARY
12. REVERSING
13. TRIAL BALANCE
14. INCOME SUMMARY

CHAPTER 5

THE COMMUNICATION OF ACCOUNTING INFORMATION

All that is literature seeks to communicate power; all that is not literature, to communicate knowledge.
Thomas de Quincey

OVERVIEW

Chapter 4 discussed the important portions of the accounting process that takes place at the end of the year. These included the adjustment process, preparation of the four basic financial statements, and the closing process which prepares the records for the next accounting period. However, this end to the internal portions of the accounting process is just the beginning of the process of communicating accounting information to external users. In this chapter, we discuss the important players in this communication process, the many statement format choices available, the additional note disclosures that are required for both private and public companies, and the process, manner, and timing of the transmission of this information to users. At the same time we discuss common uses of the information in investment analysis, debt contracts, and management compensation decisions. These discussions will help you consolidate much of what you have learned about the financial reporting process from prior chapters. They will also preview many of the important issues we will address later in the book.

LEARNING OBJECTIVES

1. Recognize the people involved in the accounting communication process (managers, auditors, information intermediaries, government regulators, and users), their roles in the process, and the guidance they receive from legal and professional standards.

2. Understand the principles and constraints that guide management and the FASB in deciding what financial information should be reported.

3. Analyze the different financial statement and disclosure formats used by companies in practice.

4. Identify the steps in the accounting communication process including issuance of press releases, annual reports, quarterly reports, and SEC filings, and the role of electronic information services in this process.

CHAPTER OUTLINE

Who is responsible for communicating accounting information?

The **managers** of the company have the primary responsibility for reported information

  •chairman and chief executive officer (CEO)

  •chief financial officer (CFO)

  •accounting staff have professional responsibility for the accuracy of the information prepared

The outside **auditors** give independent verification to the statements

  •unqualified, or clean, opinion states that information is fairly presented in conformance with generally accepted accounting principles (**GAAP**)

Outside **analysts**, working for brokerages, investment bankers, mutual fund brokers, and investment advisory services

  •gather information on companies

  •are often specialists in one industry, or company

  •prepare earnings forecasts for the company

Electronic **information services** provide information on-line, or on compact disk, to interested parties

The Securities and Exchange Commission (SEC), a **government regulator**, sets and enforces standards for reporting for companies whose stock is offered to the public

Various **users** rely on the information received from companies

  •institutional investors are the managers of pension funds, charities, trusts, mutual funds

  •private investors own shares of stock as individuals

  •creditors are interested in financial results because they have loaned money to the company

      ◊often *customers* use financial information of *suppliers* to assure reliability

What are the principles that help determine the information that should be reported?

Decision makers expect useful information; certain qualitative characteristics identified by FASB to satisfy this

- **primary qualitative** characteristics
    - ◊**relevant** information is capable of influencing decisions
    - ◊**reliable** information is accurate, unbiased, verifiable
- **secondary qualitative** characteristics
    - ◊information should be **comparable** across businesses
    - ◊information should be **consistent**, that is, it can be compared over time for the same company

Other principles and constraints also applied

- **full disclosure** principle requires
    - ◊complete set of financial statements
    - ◊explanatory footnotes
- certain **constraints** are intended to reduce volume and cost of information without decreasing value
    - ◊**materiality** constraint says that items of low significance do not have to be reported separately or conform precisely to guidelines
    - ◊**cost-benefit** constraint recognizes that the cost of providing information should not exceed the value of that information
    - ◊ **conservatism** constraint seeks to avoid overstatement of the value of assets and revenues, or understatement of liabilities and expenses
        - ·when choosing among reporting alternatives, if all other factors are equal, the one with the least positive effect on income will be chosen
    - ◊in some **industries**, certain practices are considered standard, or are required by regulatory agencies

What are the choices in the format of financial statements and disclosures?

A **classified balance sheet** separates current assets and liabilities from long term assets and liabilities, and classifies assets by type

- may be in **report form** (assets above liabilities and equity), or **account form** (assets next to liabilities and equity)
    - ◊**current assets** will be turned into cash within the longer of one year or one operating cycle

◊**long term investments** include investments in real estate not used in operations, and in other companies' stocks and bonds

◊**operational assets** (fixed assets: property, plant and equipment) are used to operate the business

·cost is apportioned over life of asset via **depreciation**

·cost less accumulated depreciation (depreciation from all past periods) equals **net book value**, or carrying value of asset

◊**intangible assets** are also noncurrent, but have no physical substance

·value comes from legal rights, privileges

◊**deferred charges** are long-term prepayments for goods and services for resale

·prepaid expenses are current prepayments

◊**current liabilities** will be paid with current assets, normally within one year

◊**long-term liabilities** have maturities beyond one year

◊**stockholders' equity** is what is left for stockholders after creditors' claims on assets are satisfied

·contributed capital plus retained earnings

∞contributed capital made up of capital stock (number of shares times par value per share) plus paid in capital in excess of par

∞par value sets a legal minimum value at which stock can be sold

A **classified income statement** identifies various types of income and may have subtotals within these sections

•income from **continuing operations**, or the company's usual business, is always the first section

◊may be done in a **single-step** format, **multiple-step**, or **multiple-step** with cost of goods sold subtracted from sales to show **gross profit**

·**net sales** are sales less any discounts, allowances or returns

·**cost of goods sold** is the cost of inventory sold to customers

·**gross margin** (gross profit) is sales less cost of goods sold

∞gross profit ratio or percentage = gross profit ÷ net sales

∞**common-sized** income statements report *all* income statement items as a percentage of sales, as a first step in analysis

100

·**operating expenses** are the everyday expenses incurred in running a business

∞**selling expense** is associated with sales activity

∞**general and administrative expense** is overall business expense

·**income from operations** is the difference between gross profit and operating expense

·**non-operating items** are those that are not the company's regular business, but are not unusual or infrequent

·**pretax earnings**, or income before income tax, = operating income - nonoperating items

•**discontinued operations** are major segments of the business that have been sold or otherwise disposed of

◊presented separately on income statement, and operating information separated from gain or loss on disposal

•**extraordinary items** consist of gains or losses that are both *unusual* and *infrequent*

•a **change in accounting method** from one acceptable method to another requires that income statement effects of changes to balance sheet accounts be disclosed in a separate section

•**earnings per share** of common stock must be disclosed in addition to total net income

◊calculated as net income ÷ weighted average shares outstanding

---

Reference point: Go back to Exhibit 5-6 in your text and review the Callaway income statement in the three formats for the operating section to be certain you see the differences. Do you see that the individual items and the net income ("bottom line") do not change, no matter which format is used?

What can be found in the footnotes to financial statements?

Descriptions of key accounting policies used by the company are provided

•needed in order to make comparisons between companies, and understand the data presented

Additional details on reported numbers are supplied

•may show revenues by geographic segment, descriptions of unusual transactions, expanded information on a line item

Some information is not disclosed in statements, but is relevant to decision makers, and thus revealed in footnotes

•includes information on legal matters, items occurring after year-end

In what ways does a company disclose information to the public?

Press releases are used to announce earnings figures as soon as they are available

•market reacts to the *difference* between actual and predicted earnings; called **unexpected earnings**

•press releases also used for new product announcements, officer changes, board changes

Annual reports are the *formal* presentation of year's results

•presentation may be limited to financial statements, footnotes, and auditors' opinion for privately held companies

•requirements are greater for public companies, and they usually wish to present a more elaborate picture

·usually have two sections: non-financial and financial

∞financial section includes statements, summarized data for five years, management discussion, footnotes, auditors' report, stock price information, summaries of unaudited quarterly data, listings of directors and officers

Quarterly reports are released in less detail than annual report

•these are unaudited, with no cash flow statement, statement of stockholders' equity, or footnotes

SEC reports include an annual report (known as **10K**), quarterly reports (**10Q**) and current event reports (**8K**)

•the **10K** provides detailed description of the business

◊includes items with no book value (thus not on the balance sheet) but with financial significance

•the **10Q** includes all quarterly report information, plus statements of stockholders' equity and cash flows, footnotes and a management discussion

•the **8K** must be filed within 15 days of any material event important to investors

QUESTIONS AND EXERCISES

Multiple Choice:

Choose the best answer to each question below, and circle the letter in front of that answer. Remember that more than one answer may be *true*, but only one is the *best* answer to the question. Think over the questions carefully.

1. The primary responsibility for the information reported by a company rests with
    a. its auditors.
    b. the accountants who prepared the information.
    c. the SEC.
    d. the company's management.
    e. the Board of Directors.

2. Many privately owned companies have their statements audited because
    a. it is required by the SEC.
    b. they will eventually be public companies.
    c. the audit opinion lends credibility to the information presented.
    d. lenders and private investors often require this.
    e. both (c) and (d).

3. The government regulatory agency that sets and enforces reporting standards for public companies is the
    a. SEC.
    b. Congress.
    c. FASB.
    d. Senate.
    e. AICPA.

4. Relevant information is
    a. information people want to know.
    b. information about current activities only.
    c. information capable of influencing decisions.
    d. information that management feels is necessary to disclose.
    e. information approved for release by the Board of Directors.

103

5. Accurate, unbiased and verifiable information is known as _____ information
   a. audited
   b. reliable
   c. relevant
   d. public
   e. consistent

6. Similar accounting methods must be applied by businesses in order for their respective financial information to be
   a. publishable.
   b. reliable.
   c. relevant.
   d. comparable.
   e. cost beneficial.

7. The cost to produce and report financial information must not exceed
   a. the benefit gained from the disclosure.
   b. a certain percentage of net income.
   c. the company's revenues.
   d. an amount set by the FASB.
   e. none of the above. All information must be reported.

8. The _____ constraint requires that care should be taken to avoid overstating revenues and assets.
   a. materiality
   b. cost-benefit
   c. relevancy
   d. conservatism
   e. full disclosure

9. The current ratio compares
   a. the relative sizes of current assets and cash.
   b. current assets to current liabilities.
   c. current assets to noncurrent assets.
   d. current assets to current liabilities and equity.
   e. the total current assets to other similar companies.

10. Operational assets include
    a. inventory.
    b. property, plant and equipment.
    c. land.
    d. intangible assets.
    e. both (b) and (c).

J. C. Penney Company, Inc., in their 1994 annual report, showed the following in footnote 3, "Properties:"

Land	$213
Buildings	
Owned	2,178
Capital leases	186
Fixtures and equipment	2,763
Leasehold improvements	611
	5,951
Less accumulated depreciation	
and amortization	1,997
Properties, net	$3,954

Use this information to answer the next 3 questions:

11. The asset for which no depreciation or amortization is included in the line item ($1,997) above is
    a. Capital leases.
    b. Leasehold improvements.
    c. Land.
    d. all of the above.
    e. none of the above—all are depreciated.

12. The total amount of depreciation expense associated with the listed assets, charged against net income since these assets were purchased, is
    a. $3,954.
    b. $1,997.
    c. $5,951.
    d. not able to be determined from the information given.
    e. $1,784.

13. The current market value of the listed assets
    a. cannot be determined from examining the information given.
    b. is $3,954.
    c. is $1,997.
    d. is $5,951.
    e. is $5,765.

14. The par value of stock is
    a. what the first person who bought the shares paid for them.
    b. an arbitrary number set by the company meaning nothing to accountants.
    c. the approximate amount the company expects to realize for newly issued stock.
    d. a legal term, setting a value below which the stock cannot be sold.
    e. equal to contributed capital.

15. Gross profit, or gross margin, is
    a. the same as net income.
    b. equal to income before taxes.
    c. another word for revenues
    d. equal to income before extraordinary items.
    e. sales less cost of goods sold.

16. Selling, general and administrative expenses are
    a. operating expenses
    b. part of the gross profit calculation.
    c. non-operating items.
    d. extraordinary items.
    e. not included in a single-step income statement.

17. Earnings per share is defined as

    a. the amount of the annual dividend paid to a shareholder on one share of stock.

    b. the amount of net income attributable to one share of common stock.

    c. the appreciation in market value of one share of stock.

    d. the amount the company receives for the sale of one share of stock.

    e. the amount a shareholder receives when selling one share of stock to another individual.

18. Information on a company's sales in the Pacific Rim would most likely

    a. not be found in the annual report.

    b. be found in one of the footnotes to the financial statements.

    c. be found in the income statement.

    d. be found in the management discussion.

    e. be found in the balance sheet.

19. Unexpected earnings are defined as

    a. net income earned when the company thought it was going to have a loss.

    b. being able to obtain a higher selling price than expected for merchandise.

    c. the difference between analysts' predicted earnings and the company's actual earnings.

    d. sales to a new market sector.

    e. earnings discovered by outside accountants during the annual audit.

20. The Form 10-Q to the SEC must include the _____, which need not be included in the company's quarterly report to investors.

    a. auditors' report

    b. statement of shareholders' equity

    c. statement of cash flows

    d. balance sheet

    e. both (b) and (c)

True or False?

For each of the following statements, place the letter "T" or "F" in the space before the statement to indicate whether you think the statement is true or false. Restate each false statement to make it true, to be sure you understand the concepts presented.

_____ 21. Only public companies go to the expense of having audited financial statements prepared.

_____ 22. Public companies are required to have their statements audited by a "Big Six" accounting firm.

_____ 23. The full disclosure principle requires a complete set of financial statements and notes to explain accounting policies, elaborate on the numbers in the statements, and disclose any items with financial significance that are not on the statements.

_____ 24. Companies in the same industry often use the same accounting policies in their published reports.

_____ 25. Operating assets, like any other asset, are intended to eventually be sold and turned into cash.

_____ 26. An example of an extraordinary item would be a leak in a furnace necessitating an especially expensive repair to the furnace.

_____ 27. Information may be reliable but not material.

_____ 28. The conservatism constraint recognizes that the cost of providing information should not exceed the benefit of having the information available.

_____ 29. Common-sized income statements report all items as a percentage of net income.

_____ 30. A change in accounting method requires restatement of prior years as though the new method had always been in place.

A Few Words from You ...

Answer each of the following with a short discussion of the issues involved, or appropriate calculations.

31. **Do actions speak as well as words?**   During the Summer of 1995, an article in *The Wall Street Journal* [2] noted that Callaway Golf was rumored to be a takeover target. There was no press release commenting on these rumors. However, the article noted, in the past few weeks corporate managers were purchasing significant numbers of shares, and the company bought back shares from its founder, Ely Callaway. They also adopted a rights offering to existing stockholders, and a share-repurchase program. What message is the company sending to investors and potential investors by these actions? What effect would you expect this to have on the company's stock price? Would a takeover be of interest to investors?

32. **Why is this extraordinary?** The Caldor Corporation, in its year ended January 29, 1994, shows an "Extraordinary loss on early retirement of debt" of $5,378,000 on its Income Statement.   Why do you think this is considered an extraordinary item?

---

[2]Kansas, Dave, "Callaway's Buying Chips Takeover Talk," *The Wall Street Journal,* July 5, 1995.

33. Can you recognize this statement?

Kellogg Company had the following statement in its 1993 Annual Report:

Consolidated Earnings and Retained Earnings

Year ended December 31, (in millions, except per share amounts)	1993
Net sales	$6,295.4
Other revenue (deductions), net	(1.5)
Cost of goods sold	2,989.0
Selling and administrative expense	2,237.5
Interest expense	33.3
Earnings before income taxes	1,034.1
Income taxes	353.4
Net earnings—$2.94 a share	680.7
Retained earnings, beginning of year	3,033.9
Dividends paid—$1.32 a share	(305.2)
Retained earnings, end of year	$3,409.4

What statement(s) is this? Is this presentation incorrect? Does it convey the information clearly and adequately?

What format is the statement in? On what do you base your answer?

Recast the statement in one of the other formats you learned. Does this make it any more useful to you? Discuss briefly the decision process a company might go through in deciding how to present information in their annual report.

34. **How do investors view the company's pubic conscience?** J. C. Penney Company, Inc. has a section of their 1994 Annual Report entitled "Public Affairs," containing such items as Community Relations, Minority and Women-owned Businesses, Environmental Affairs and Independent Board of Directors, among others. What relationship does this have to the company's financial status? Review in your text the typical content of an annual report. How does this fit in? Is it important to investors? Explain.

35. **What does the memo portion of the line item mean?** Wal-Mart Stores, Inc. in their 1994 Annual Report showed the following:

Common stock ($.10 par value; 5,500,000 shares authorized, 2,298,769 issued and outstanding)

What dollar amount would be given for the "Common stock" line on the balance sheet (they round to thousands)?

Their paid-in capital in excess of par was shown as $535,639. (In $000) What was the average amount per share obtained for issued stock? Is this the amount you could expect to pay for a share of stock if you tried to buy one now? Explain.

How many more shares can the company issue without having to go back to the shareholders for approval? What is the importance of this figure?

Explain the meaning of their phrase, "issued and outstanding."

Team up!

Get together in teams of 3 - 5 members to decide each of the following:

36. **What is in a news release?** Look through a current issue of *The Wall Street Journal* . Find three or four articles that are based on press releases from companies. Try to find a variety of items, not just a stack of articles, all on quarterly earnings. For each one, answer the following:

What information was the press release intended to convey? Was it positive, or not so?

How did the writer of the article appear to you to respond to the information? Did they appear to have a favorable or unfavorable *opinion* (beyond strict reporting of the facts)?

How did the "market" respond to the news, based on what the article tells you? Do you agree with the response, or would your opinion be somewhat different? Why?

If possible, obtain a copy of the complete text of one of the news releases chose. Was there any additional information in the complete text that would change your opinion of the announcement, from the impression you formed by just reading the article? Explain.

37. **How are accounting principles and concepts applied?** Use the Annual Report for Toys "R" Us in your textbook to find a specific example of the application of each of the following:

Comparability:

Consistency:

Full disclosure:

Conservatism:

Continuity:

Time-period assumption:

Unit-of-measure assumption:

Matching:

And just for the fun of it ...

The word block below contains a complete financial statement for a public company. All the information except the numbers is contained here, but not in the correct order. You must sort out the words, beginning with the name of the company (that, at least, should be easy to find). Phrases (such as "retained earnings") and logical line titles ("accrued federal and state income taxes") are kept together. The answer key supplies the numbers, too, in case you are interested.

	O	t	h	e	r	i	n	c	o	m	e	-	n	e	t	O	p
e	r	a	t	i	n	g	,	s	e	l	l	i	n	g	,	a	n
d	g	e	n	e	r	a	l	a	d	m	i	n	i	s	t	r	a
t	i	v	e	e	x	p	e	n	s	e	s		W	a	l	-	M
a	r	t	S	t	o	r	e	s	,	I	n	c	.	a	n	d	S
u	b	s	i	d	i	a	r	i	e	s	D	e	f	e	r	r	e
d		I	n	t	e	r	e	s	t	c	o	s	t	s	:	D	e
b	t	R	e	v	e	n	u	e	s	:	C	o	s	t	o	f	s
a	l	e	s	N	e	t	s	a	l	e	s	I	n	c	o	m	e
B	e	f	o	r	e	I	n	c	o	m	e	T	a	x	e	s	
C	o	s	t	s	a	n	d	E	x	p	e	n	s	e	s	:	C
o	n	s	o	l	i	d	a	t	e	d	S	t	a	t	e	m	e
n	t	s	o	f	I	n	c	o	m	e	C	a	p	i	t	a	l
l	e	a	s	e	s		N	e	t	I	n	c	o	m	e	F	i
s	c	a	l	y	e	a	r	e	n	d	e	d	J	a	n	u	a
r	y	3	1	,	1	9	9	4		R	e	n	t	a	l	s	f
r	o	m	l	i	c	e	n	s	e	d	d	e	p	a	r	t	m
e	n	t	s	P	r	o	v	i	s	i	o	n	f	o	r	I	n
c	o	m	e	T	a	x	e	s	:	C	u	r	r	e	n	t	

SOLUTIONS

Multiple Choice:

1. (d) 2. (e) 3. (a) 4. (c) 5. (b) 6. (d) 7. (a) 8. (d) 9. (b) 10. (e) 11. (c) 12. (b) 13. (a) 14. (d) 15. (e) 16. (a) 17. (b) 18. (b) 19. (c) 20. (e)

True or false:

21. False. All companies at some time may need audited statements, to lend credibility to the information presented.

22. False. Public companies are required to have their statements audited by a public accounting firm, not necessarily "Big Six."

23. True.

24. True.

25. False. Operating asset are intended for use in running the business, not to be sold.

26. False. The leak in the furnace would be a repair to an operating asset. Although very expensive, this event is not particularly unusual.

27. True.

28. False. The conservatism constraint avoids overstating assets or understating liabilities. The item described is the cost-benefit principle.

29. False. Common-sized income statements report all items as a percentage of *sales* .

30. True.

And just for the fun of it: (amounts in $000)

Wal-Mart Stores, Inc. and Subsidiaries
Consolidated Statements of Income
Fiscal year ended January 31, 1994

Revenues:

Net Sales	$67,344,574
Rentals from licensed departments	47,422
Other income—net	593,548
	67,985,544

Costs and Expenses:

Cost of sales	53,443,743
Operating, selling and general and administrative expenses	10,333,218

Interest Costs:

Debt	331,308
Capital leases	185,697
	64,293,966
Income Before Income Taxes	3,691,578

Provision for Income Taxes:

Current	1,324,777
Deferred	33,524
	1,358,301
Net Income	$2,333,277

CHAPTER 6

ACCOUNTING FOR SALES REVENUE, CASH, AND RECEIVABLES

He [Alexander Hamilton] smote the rock of the national resources, and abundant streams of revenue gushed forth. He touched the dead corpse of the Public Credit, and it sprung upon its feet.
Daniel Webster

OVERVIEW

In this chapter, we begin our in-depth discussion of the financial statements. We will begin with two of the most liquid assets, cash and accounts receivable, and transactions that involve revenue, adjustments to revenues, and certain selling expenses that relate to recording cash and accounts receivable. Accuracy in revenue recognition and the related recognition of cost of goods sold (discussed in the next chapter) are thought by many analysts and the SEC to be the most important determinants of the accuracy and thus the usefulness of financial statement presentations. We also introduce concepts related to the management and control of cash and receivables, which is a critical business function. A detailed understanding of these topics is crucial to future managers, accountants, and financial analysts.

LEARNING OBJECTIVES

1. Apply the revenue principle to determine the appropriate time to record sales revenue for typical retailers, wholesalers, and manufacturers.

2. Determine the appropriate amount to report as net sales when there are cash sales, credit card sales, credit sales (and sales discounts), and sales returns.

3. Estimate, account for, and report the effects of uncollectible accounts receivable (bad debts) on the financial statements.

4. Apply the revenue principle to special circumstances including deferred revenues, installment sales, and long-term construction and service contracts.

5. Report, control, and safeguard cash.

CHAPTER OUTLINE

How is the revenue principle applied to sales?

The **revenue principle** requires that revenues be recognized when earned, no matter when cash is exchanged

> •for most companies, recognition occurs when merchandise is *shipped*
>
> •**cash equivalent** sales price is usually proper *amount* to recognize

How does the form of payment affect the amount of revenue recorded?

When a **cash sale** takes place, the amount of revenue is simply the cash (or check) received

> •results in a debit to cash, a credit to sales (revenue)

Credit card sales : bank credit cards, not the retailer's own

> •they provide some advantages to retailers
>
> > ◊increases the number of people willing to shop at the establishment
> >
> > ◊avoids costs of retailer providing credit
> >
> > ◊avoids losses from bad checks—credit card issuer assumes collection responsibility
> >
> > ◊collect cash faster than would happen if the store provided credit itself
>
> •usually the retailer is charged a fee—the **credit card discount**—for these sales by the bank that issued the card
>
> > ◊fee is commonly about 2 percent of the sale; when credit card receipt is deposited at retailer's bank, cash received is 2 percent less than the amount of sale
> >
> > > ·may be recorded as a **contra revenue** account, or as an addition to **selling expense**

Credit sales involve shipping merchandise to customers, billing them, and granting a "credit period"

> •the credit period is a certain length of time to pay, generally 30 days
>
> •a **sales discount**, often called a cash discount, is often granted to encourage early payment
>
> > ◊customers are allowed to pay somewhat less than full invoice if they pay within 10 days, for example

◊may be recorded as **contra revenue**, or **selling expense**

◊usually record sale at gross amount, and discount when customer takes it

◊not the same as a **trade discount**, which is an amount deducted from listed price for volume sales, or for hastening the sale of slow-moving merchandise

·these sales are recorded at the *net* amount, after discount

When customers return merchandise for any reason, a **sales returns and allowances** account is debited

•*contra revenue* account that lets company know how satisfied customers are with the merchandise they receive

Net sales on the income statement is sales less: returns and allowances, sales discounts, and credit card discounts

What is an account receivable?

A **receivable** is a claim for cash, goods, or services

•an **account receivable** is created when there is a credit sale on open account

•a **note receivable** is a written promise to pay a specified *sum of money* on a known *maturity date* , and specified *interest* at one or more future dates

◊**principal** is the amount borrowed

◊**interest** is money charged for use of principal

•a **trade receivable** is created in the normal course of business, selling goods or services

•a **non-trade receivable** is for transactions other than sale of goods or services

•receivables are also either **current** (short term, or less than one year) or **noncurrent** (long term, or extending beyond one year)

How are bad debts accounted for?

A bad debt is created when a customer account cannot be collected

•bad debt expense is the expense associated with *estimated* uncollectible accounts

◊should be matched with (recorded in) the same period as the related sales

·company knows that some credit customers may not ultimately be able to pay their credit accounts, no matter how carefully credit accounts are given

·company may not find out about this inability to pay until the accounting period *after* the sale

·the **allowance method** is used to determine bad debt expense related to this period's sales

What are the two steps involved in the allowance method for measuring bad debt expense?

It is not always possible to know in advance *who will not be able to pay* or *when the bad debts will become obvious* ; thus the allowance method is used

> •first an **estimate** is made of the amount of bad debts that will result from the current period's credit sales

> •an *adjusting journal entry* is made at the end of the period to record this estimate, with the **debit** to **bad debt expense** and the **credit** to a **contra asset** account known as the **allowance for doubtful accounts** (or allowance for bad debts, or allowance for uncollectible accounts)

>> ◊cannot credit accounts receivable because no *known* account is currently uncollectible

>> ◊allowance is deducted from accounts receivable to determine amount expected to be turned into cash; thus

>>> Accounts receivable
>>> - Allowance for doubtful accounts
>>> = Accounts receivable, net (net realizable value, or net book value)

How is a specific uncollectible account written off?

Specific accounts are written off with journal entries throughout the year

> •allowance was established to absorb specific accounts

> •debit is made to allowance account

> •credit is made to accounts receivable

>> ◊no income statement accounts affected (income statement was reduced when bad debts adjusting entry was made in period of sale)

>> ◊net realizable accounts receivable does not change because reduction in accounts receivable is offset by reduction in contra account (allowance)

What if a payment is received from a customer whose account was previously written off?

If an account previously written off pays after all, the account must be reinstated

> •customer's account is restored by reversing write-off entry: debit accounts receivable, credit the allowance

•payment is recorded as usual: debit cash, credit accounts receivable

What is accounts receivable turnover?

Receivables turnover measures effectiveness of credit policy and collections

   •calculated by: **net credit sales ÷ average accounts receivable**

   •if it deteriorates, or compares badly to similar companies, this might indicate granting of credit to poor credit risks or ineffective collection efforts

How does a company estimate its bad debt expense?

A company may use a **percentage of credit sales** to estimate bad debts

   •divide total historical bad debt losses by total credit sales

   •company needs a few years' history to predict the future

      ◊new company may rely on experience of similar companies

An alternate method is the **aging of accounts receivable** method

   •the older an account is, the less likely it is to be collectible

   •sort accounts receivable by how long they have been outstanding

   •for each range, develop an estimated percentage that will be uncollectible (based on experience)

   •this percentage, times the dollar amount in the group, equals estimated uncollectible accounts for that group

   •the total for all groups is the amount that should be the *balance of the allowance account*

   ### •Note the difference in the two methods:

      ◊the **percentage of sales method** calculates **bad debt expense directly**

      ◊the **aging of accounts receivable** method calculates the **ending balance of the allowance** for doubtful accounts, and bad debt expense is then calculated by comparing the difference between this ending balance, and the existing balance in the account

How does the revenue principle apply to deferred revenues?

If cash is collected before goods or services are delivered earnings process is incomplete, revenues not earned

   •liability recorded for **unearned (deferred) revenues**

121

•adjusting entry made at the end of a year for the portion of unearned revenue earned as of that date

How does the revenue principle apply to installment sales?

When goods or services are delivered but payment is uncertain, revenue recognition is delayed until collection is made; called **installment method**

•very conservative, only applied under special circumstances of uncertainty

Are there exceptions to the revenue recognition criteria?

Long term construction projects, for example the construction of a building, would have no revenue for a number of years because of the length of time they take to complete, and then a massive amount in the year of completion

•this method of recognition is called the **completed contract method**

•companies often use the **percentage of completion method**, where revenues are recorded based on the percentage of the total work completed during the period

◊typically this total work is calculated based on total cost, so percentage if completion equals

$$\frac{\text{cost incurred this period}}{\text{total cost for contract}}$$

◊note that earnings process is not complete; however underlying economic activity is better represented by this method

Service contracts that cover more than one accounting period also commonly use the **percentage of completion** method

•also referred to as **proportional performance** method

What is the difference between cash and cash equivalents?

Cash is money or any instrument a bank will accept for deposit and immediately credit to depositor's account

•divided between cash on hand, cash deposited in banks, and other instruments that meet definition of cash

Cash equivalents are investments with maturities of three months or less, readily convertible to cash, whose value is unlikely to change

What internal control procedures are necessary to safeguard cash?

Cash is the asset most vulnerable to fraud and theft; control involves

122

•separation of duties: separation of receipts and disbursements; separation of accounting for both; separation of handling and accounting for cash

•individual responsibility: daily cash deposits; petty cash control; approvals of expenditures; payment approvals and check signing; monthly reconciliation of bank accounts

SUPPLEMENT A
RECONCILIATION OF THE CASH ACCOUNTS AND THE BANK STATEMENTS

How is a bank statement reconciled to the books of account?

A bank sends a monthly **bank statement** to a depositor showing the activity in each account held by the depositor at that bank: deposits, checks cleared, balances, bank service charges

> •**reconciliation** is the process of calculating ending cash balance in company's records and ending balance per the bank, and identifying (and recording if necessary) differences between the two
>
> > ◊this serves to check accuracy of both bank and books of account, and identifies any corrections necessary
> >
> > ◊some items recorded by depositor had not reached bank by date of statement: outstanding checks, deposits in transit, errors
> >
> > ◊some items recorded by bank not yet known and recorded by depositor: service charges, bad checks, credit memos, errors
> >
> > ◊when all of these items are accounted for in the proper place (books of account or bank statement), the balances should equal; this balance is the one to report on the balance sheet

SUPPLEMENT B
PETTY CASH

What is petty cash and what controls are necessary?

Petty cash is a quantity of cash held at a business office so that small daily expenditures do not require the writing of checks

> •check to "petty cash" is written and cashed
>
> •money is kept in a safe place and replenished when necessary

123

•disbursements made with proper documentation or receipts for small expenditures
•replenished by writing a check for exact amount of receipted expenditures, crediting cash and debiting various expenses (per receipts)

QUESTIONS AND EXERCISES

Multiple Choice:

For each question below you are to choose the best of the five possible answers.
Remember that more than one may be a *possible* answer, but *only one* is the best .

1. The credit card discount is

   a. the amount off the list price of an item that the merchant allows a credit card customer.

   b. the amount off the list price that service stations, who do not want to have as many credit sales, offer to cash customers.

   c. the amount the issuing bank charges a retailer as a handling fee for each credit card sale submitted for payment.

   d. an amount paid by the issuing bank to retailers to encourage the use of their credit cards.

   e. the amount saved by a credit card holder who pays credit card bills in full by their due date.

2. Sales discounts, also called cash discounts, are often granted to

   a. encourage credit customers to pay invoices early.

   b. encourage customers to buy slow-moving merchandise.

   c. give favorable terms to high-volume buyers.

   d. discourage bad debts.

   e. increase the gross profit percentage.

3. Sales on which there is a trade discount are normally recorded

   a. at the gross amount, with an offsetting contra account.

   b. at the net amount, after the discount is deducted.

   c. at the gross amount, with the discount in an expense account.

   d. either a or b.

   e. either b or c.

4. The primary difference between an account receivable and a note receivable is

    a. a note is backed up by a written document, but an account receivable is not.

    b. a note receivable is legally binding, but an account receivable is not.

    c. an account receivable can only be recorded for sales of goods and services.

    d. an account receivable is a current asset, whereas a note is a long-term asset.

    e. a note receivable generally carries an interest charge, whereas an account receivable generally does not.

5. The primary reason for not writing off bad debts when they actually become uncollectible, as opposed to establishing an allowance account, is

    a. an allowance account simplifies the bookkeeping.

    b. it might be too easy to ignore these overdue accounts if there were no allowance.

    c. the allowance accounts results in a more accurate representation of revenues on the income statement.

    d. the allowance method results in a correct application of the matching principle, whereas the direct write-off method does not.

    e. it is done by most companies with substantial accounts receivable.

6. Balluster Company, which uses the allowance method, estimated that their bad debt expense for the most recent year-end should be $10,000. They should record this as follows:

    a. Bad debt expense   10,000
         Accounts receivable   10,000

    b. Bad debt expense   10,000
         Allowance for doubtful accounts   10,000

    c. Allowance for doubtful accounts   10,000
         Bad debt expense   10,000

    d. Bad debt expense   10,000
         Cash   10,000

    e. Bad debt expense   10,000
         Accounts payable   10,000

7. When a customer owing Balluster Company (see question 6) goes bankrupt, they decide to write off the outstanding balance of $2,000 in the account. The correct entry for this is

    a. Bad debt expense   2,000
           Accounts receivable   2,000

    b. Bad debt expense   2,000
           Accounts payable   2,000

    c. Allowance for doubtful accounts   2,000
           Accounts receivable   2,000

    d. Allowance for doubtful accounts   2,000
           Bad debt expense   2,000

    e. Sales   2,000
           Accounts receivable   2,000

8. Kellogg Company showed the following for 1993, according to their Annual Report ($millions):

    Net sales $6295.4
    Accounts receivable   536.8

Their accounts receivable turnover was

    a. 8.5
    b. 9%
    c. 11.7
    d. 12%
    e. cannot be determined from this information.

The next three questions (8–10) are based on the following 1993 data taken in part from the Annual Report of Whirlpool Corporation, using actual figures where available. All amounts are in millions of dollars.

Accounts Receivable				Allowance for doubtful accounts	
beg. 886					35 beg.
sales 7368			write-offs 36		
	7352 collections				

9. Suppose Whirlpool uses the percentage of credit sales method for estimating bad debts. For the current year they assume that 1/2 percent (.005) of their credit sales will be uncollectible. Their bad debt expense will be _____ and the ending balance of the Allowance account will be _____.

      a. 37; 36
      b. 36; 37
      c. 35; 1
      d. 4; 3
      e. 6; 5

10. Alternatively, assume that Whirlpool uses the aging of accounts receivable method. For this year-end they assume that a cumulative weighted total of 4 percent of accounts receivable will be uncollectible. Bad debt expense will therefore be _____ and the ending balance of the allowance will be

      a. 6; 5
      b. 4; 3
      c. 35; 1
      d. 36; 37
      e. 37; 36

11. The net book value of Whirlpool's accounts receivable at the end of 1993 is
   a. 902
   b. 866
   c. 886
   d. 851
   e. 865

12. General Electric Company, in their 1993 Annual Report, states the following:

   Premiums on short-duration insurance contracts are reported
   as earned income over the terms of the related reinsurance
   treaties or insurance policies.

This is an example of
   a. the installment method.
   b. the percentage-of-completion method.
   c. deferred revenues.
   d. the completed contract method.
   e. an extraordinary item.

13. The Boeing Company reports in a footnote to its 1993 Annual Report:

   For certain fixed-price contracts that require substantial
   performance over a long time period before deliveries begin,
   sales are recorded based upon attainment of scheduled
   performance milestones.

This is an example of
   a. recognizing revenue upon delivery of goods or services.
   b. the completed contract method.
   c. deferred revenues.
   d. the percentage-of-completion method.
   e. the installment method.

14. When you returned to school in September, you immediately began to research air fares to your home for the winter vacation. You found an airline willing to sell you a ticket at almost 60% below the usual rate, but you must follow some restrictions (such as leaving and returning on a non-holiday weekday, and staying a minimum number of days) and you had to buy your ticket before October 1.

You immediately purchased your ticket. Assuming both you and the airline keep accrual basis books of account, you have a(n) _____ and the airline has a(n) _____ .

    a. asset; revenue

    b. expense; revenue

    c. expense; asset

    d. expense; liability

    e. asset; liability

15. A U. S. government treasury bill owned by a company, maturing in two months, would be classified on the balance sheet as

    a. cash.

    b. petty cash.

    c. a cash equivalent.

    d. a long-term investment.

    e. a short-term investment.

16. On a recent trip to the local Acura dealership for some tune-up parts, Bill gave his list of requested parts to a clerk in the parts department. The clerk gathered the parts together and prepared a computer-generated list with prices to accompany the package. He then stapled the parts into a bag with the list attached to the outside and sent them to the front desk clerk, where the sale was rung into the cash register and Bill collected the package and paid. The internal control procedure in evidence here is

    a. separation of duties.

    b. separation of accounting procedures.

    c. inventory control.

    d. reconciliation of cash.

    e. employee cross-training.

17. The most important reason to reconcile the company's bank statement each month is
    a. to make sure that the bank is not making errors.
    b. that if it is let go for more than one month, it is very time consuming to catch up.
    c. to ensure that cash is being properly accounted for and safeguarded.
    d. it is required by GAAP.
    e. it is the only way to know how much cash is really available to pay bills.

18. A credit memo in a bank statement is usually
    a. a bank service charge.
    b. a note receivable collected by the bank for the depositor.
    c. a memo returning a NSF check.
    d. the correction of an error.
    e. a deposit made at the bank.

19. The reimbursement of a petty cash fund is
    a. usually about $100.
    b. equal to the sum of the receipts for the disbursements made from it.
    c. equal to an amount deemed adequate for the next day's needs by the petty cash custodian.
    d. done monthly, on the last day of the month.
    e. done weekly.

20. A company's primary source of cash is
    a. the sale of goods or services and the collection of accounts receivable.
    b. the issue of new shares of the company's stock.
    c. borrowings on long-term debt contracts.
    d. the sale of investments.
    e. short-term lines of credit.

True or False?

For each of the following statements, place the letter "T" or "F" in the space before the statement to indicate whether you think the statement is true or false. Why are the false statements not true? Reword them to make them true.

_____ 21. The revenue recognition principle requires that revenues be recorded when earned. This is always when goods pass from the seller to the buyer, or services are completed.

_____ 22. In a credit card sale, the merchant receives the cash for the sale as soon as the credit card issuer receives payment from the customer.

_____ 23. Sales revenue should always be recorded net of any trade discount.

_____ 24. "Sales discounts and allowances" is a contra revenue account.

_____ 25. Bad debts arise when a company's credit policy is too loose, or collection efforts are not vigorous enough.

_____ 26. Bad debt expense should be recorded in the period in which the corresponding sales are made, not in the period in which a particular account is actually judged uncollectible.

_____ 27. In the aging of accounts receivable method, specific accounts in each age category are identified as potentially uncollectible, and their amounts are added to the Allowance for Uncollectible Accounts.

_____ 28. The dollar amount, or percentage, of credit sales in a period considered unlikely to be ultimately turned into cash is charged to bad debit expense.

_____ 29. The net realizable value of accounts receivable consists of accounts receivable less the allowance for bad debts.

_____ 30. The installment method is a very conservative method of revenue recognition that takes into account the uncertainty of collection of the full amount of certain types of sales.

_____ 31. For a very small business, it is adequate to make bank deposits of cash and checks once a week, as long as these items are kept in a secure location in the meantime.

● A Few Words from You ...

Answer each of the following with a short discussion or appropriate calculations.

32. **Some kind of pastry??** Refer to multiple choice question 8. Explain what receivables turnover means to the Kellogg Company. What does it mean to outside parties?

33. **Why don't they come out the same every time?** The following information is available for Rainbow Sales Company for 1995:

Accounts receivable aging:

		Amounts due		
Client	<30 days	30–60	60–90	90–120	>120 days
F. E. Red	500				
B. Orange	600	100			
L. Yellow	200				
P. Green					1,400
S. Blue		300			
M. Indigo		400			
S. Violet				100	
E. Brown	100	500			
J. Black		800			
L. White	200		300		
TOTALS:	_____	_____	_____	_____	_____
bad debt rates	.005	.0075	.02	.25	.75

The estimated rates of bad debts below the aging columns were developed based on the company's past experience. The company currently uses the percentage-of-credit-sales method for estimating bad debt expense. The percentage they have been using, again based

on past experience, is 1.5 percent, or .015. They are considering a switch to the aging of
accounts receivable method. Accounts receivable at the beginning of this year had a
balance of $4800, and the allowance for uncollectible accounts began with a balance of
$546. Sales for this year, all on account, were $41,800. Collections were $40,600.

a. Total the columns in the chart and organize the data given in the chart and the paragraph
on the T-accounts below:

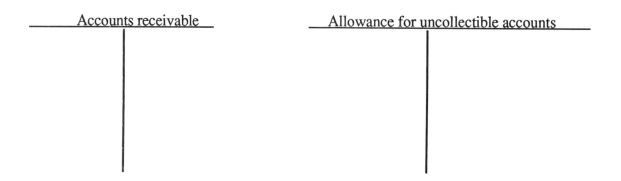

| Accounts receivable | Allowance for uncollectible accounts |

b. Calculate the dollar amount of accounts written off during the year.

c. Using the percentage-of-credit-sales method, calculate bad debt expense for the current
year, and the ending balance of the Allowance, and post your answers to the T-accounts.
Don't forget to calculate an ending balance for accounts receivable.

d. Recopy your T-accounts through step (b). Recalculate bad debt expense using the aging of accounts receivable method, and the ending balance of the Allowance, and complete the new T-accounts.

Accounts receivable	Allowance for uncollectible accounts

e. Explain your results. Why are the numbers different, if you began with the same data in both cases? Which is correct? Which is better? Explain why you got different results, and what Rainbow should consider in their decision about the method to choose.

34. **What does an internal control document look like?** Explain the internal control function each of these simple, familiar documents serves for the entity that uses them:

a. The receipt you are given by the teller when you make a deposit at your bank.

b. The piece of paper you fill out when you obtain a reimbursement from "petty cash" for a small expenditure for your employer.

c. Your copy of a credit card receipt.

d. The time card you fill out for your employer.

e. (This is a tricky one) The Form 1099 that a company sends you at the end of a year, listing miscellaneous income they paid to you as a non-employee.

35. **How do you record a billion dollars?** *The Wall Street Journal* [3] in an article in July, 1995, outlined a $1 billion, 5-year agreement announced by United Parcel Service and J. C. Penney Company, whereby UPS will become the preferred carrier for all goods shipped to Penney, and will deliver goods to customers for Penney. It is said to be the largest such contract ever in the delivery industry.

Explain the revenue recognition issues in this deal. Is the $1 billion a firm number? What is the real revenue? When will it be recorded?

Is this an item that you would expect to see in a footnote to the Annual Report of either organization? Explain.

---

[3]Frank, Robert, "UPS to Receive $1 Billion Pact From Penney," *The Wall Street Journal ,* July 11, 1995.

Team up!

Get together in teams of 3 - 5 members to work on the following problems.

36. **How do bad debt entries affect the financial statements?** The following information is available from the 1993 Annual Report of General Electric Company:

	1993	1992
Accounts Receivable	8731	7640
Allowance for losses	(170)	(178)
Current receivables	8561	7462

Design an example, using this data and hypothetical numbers of your own, that you can use to show the balance sheet and income statement effect (increase, decrease, no effect) of each of the following:

a. the entry to record bad debt expense

b. the entry to write off a specific customer account that has been judged uncollectible

c. the entry to reinstate an account previously written off, and record the payment received

As you prepare your example, keep in mind that you are trying to explain these concepts to someone who does not understand them at all. Present your example to another group, or to your entire class.

37. **Where can a company find enough employees to carry out internal control procedures?** Imagine a small company. The accounting department consists of a Controller and two clerical employees. The President and the Marketing Director are the only other officers. There are also two technical staff, and a lead technician to supervise them. Re-read the guidelines for the internal control of cash. Design a simple system for this company to properly account for and safeguard cash, keeping in mind their personnel limitations. Now, exchange your results with another group. The task of each group is to find the weaknesses in the other group's internal control system. If time allows, each group should try to correct the flaws in their design.

38. **$10 down and $10 a month?** Look through your local newspaper or canvas the neighborhood of your school. Find a business selling goods on the installment method. Describe the business, its products, and its customers.

What is it about the nature of the business or what it sells that makes collection of the accounts uncertain?

Can you think of a point in time before the entire account is paid off when the business might begin to recognize at least some revenue? Explain.

● If possible, talk with a knowledgeable manager at the business. What is their revenue recognition policy? What do they do to increase the likelihood of collection? Can you offer them any suggestions for improvement in their system?

And just for the fun of it ...

Accounting trivia ...

The quote at the beginning of the chapter mentions Alexander Hamilton. Do you know who he was? What does he have to do with the business world?

●

And just in case some of the examples seem trivial ...

Just how much do companies estimate they will lose to bad debts? Here are the allowances for bad debts for some well-known companies:

Nike, Inc.	(1993)	$19,447,000
AMR Corp. (American Airlines)	(1992)	$32,000,000
Hershey Foods	(1993)	$12,500,000
General Electric	(1993)	$170,000,000
Lotus Development Corp.	(1993)	$30,002,000

Remember, this is **cash** owed to the company that they think they will **never collect**!

●

SOLUTIONS

Multiple Choice:

1. (c) 2. (a) 3. (b) 4. (e) 5. (d) 6. (b) 7. (c) 8. (c) 9. (a) 10. (e) 11. (b) 12. (c) 13. (d) 14. (e) 15. (c) 16. (a) 17. (c) 18. (b) 19. (b) 20. (a)

True or false:

21. False. Revenues must be earned to be recorded as revenues, but this does not always happen at the point when goods or services are delivered. Long-term contracts are an example of an exception.

22. False. The merchant receives cash (or it is credited to the merchant's account) as soon as the credit card receipt is deposited with the merchant's bank.

23. True.

24. True.

25. False. Bad debts may arise any time a company grants credit to customers, no matter how carefully customer credit history is screened, or how committed the collection effort is.

26. True.

27. False. The aging of accounts receivable separates receivables into categories by their age. It still cannot point to specific accounts that definitely will go bad, but can only estimate percentages of possible defaults in each category.

28. False. This is a subtle point, hinging on one word. Many students confuse the words debts and debits. The correct term is bad DEBT expense. A debit is a left-side entry.

29. True.

30. True.

31. False. Any business, no matter the size, should make deposits daily. This is a fundamental control procedure for cash.

A few words from you:

33. a. Totals are 1600 + 2100 + 300 + 100 + 1400 = 5500 total accounts receivable

Accounts receivable			Allowance for uncollectible accounts	
beg. 4800				546 beg.
sales 41,800				
	40,600 collected		"x" = write-offs	
	"x" = write-offs			
end 5500				

b. Write-offs: 4800 + 41,800 - 40,600 - x = 5500

$$500 = x$$

c. 41800 * .015 = 627   end balance = 546 + 627 - 500 = 673

Accounts receivable			Allowance for uncollectible accounts	
beg. 4800				546 beg.
sales 41,800				
	40,600 collected		write-offs 500	
	500 write-offs			627 est. expense
end 5500				673 end

d.

Accounts receivable			Allowance for uncollectible accounts	
beg. 4800				546 beg.
sales 41,800				
	40,600 collected		write-offs 500	
	500 write-offs			1059 est. exp.
end 5500				1105 end

141

Using the percentages of aged accounts receivable:

(1600*.005) (2100*.0075) + (300*.02) + (100*.25) + 1400*.75) =

$$\text{ending balance, allowance}$$

1104.75 = ending balance

expense: 546 - 500 + y = 1105

$$y = 1059$$

And just for the fun of it:

Alexander Hamilton, born in 1757, was the first Secretary of the Treasury of the newly formed United States of America. An advocate of strong central government, he proposed among other things the levying of an excise tax to provide revenue for the government, and the absorption by the national government of state debts in connection with the Revolution. He recommended the establishment of a national bank of the U.S. and argued for protective tariffs to preserve the home market. Hamilton warned of the dangers of continuing an agrarian economy. He urged the increased development of manufacturing concerns, and import duties to protect their products from foreign competition. All these strengthened the federal government at the expense of the states. His policies became known as Hamiltonian economics. His strong economic views were his eventual undoing when he was challenged to, and killed in, a duel with long-time adversary Aaron Burr in 1804. Do any of his views sound familiar?

CHAPTER 7

MEASURING INVENTORY AND COST OF GOODS SOLD

First to come and last to go.
Henry Wadsworth Longfellow

OVERVIEW

Closely related to recording revenue is recording the cost of what was sold. This chapter focuses on transactions related to inventory and cost of goods sold. Cost of goods sold has a major impact on a company's gross profit and net income, which are closely watched by investors, analysts, and other users of financial statements. Increasing emphases on quality, productivity, and cost have further focused production managers' attention on cost of goods sold and inventory. Since inventory cost figures play a major role in product introduction and pricing decisions, they are also important to marketing and general managers. Finally, since inventory accounting has a major effect on many companies' tax liabilities, this is an important place to introduce the effect of taxation on management decision making and financial reporting.

LEARNING OBJECTIVES

1. Apply the cost principle to identify the amounts that should be included in inventory and the matching principle to determine cost of goods sold for typical retailers, wholesalers, and manufacturers.

2. Measure the effects of inventory errors on financial statements.

3. Use the four inventory costing methods to determine the appropriate amounts to report as inventory and cost of goods sold.

4. Decide when the use of different inventory costing methods is beneficial to a company.

5. Analyze financial statements prepared using different inventory costing methods.

6. Apply the lower-of-cost-or-market (LCM) rule.

7. Keep track of inventory quantities and amounts in different circumstances.

CHAPTER OUTLINE

What are the primary goals of inventory management, and what role does accounting play?

The primary **goals of inventory management** are to have **sufficient quantities** of inventory to satisfy customers' needs while **minimizing the costs** of carrying inventory.

- accurate information needed
- up-to-date information needed
- information necessary to protect assets

What is included in inventory?

Inventory is property held for resale, or to be used in producing goods or services for sale

- **merchandise inventory** is goods held for resale by a **merchandiser** (wholesaler or retailer)
- **manufacturers**, who convert inventory into goods and services for sale, hold three types
  - ◊**raw materials** are items acquired for processing into other goods
  - ◊**work in process** are goods at some stage of the manufacturing process
  - ◊**finished goods** are items completed and ready to sell
- inventory is recorded at historical cost
  - ◊all costs incurred in acquisition of inventory, up to point of being ready to use or ship to customer
    - ·often costs other than invoice cost of merchandise are not material and are expensed rather than included in inventory

What is the flow of inventory from purchase to sale?

For a merchandiser, inventory flows simply from purchase, to inventory, to cost of goods sold

For a manufacturer, inventory flows through more steps

- purchases go into raw materials inventory
- raw materials flow into work in process, where direct manufacturing labor and overhead are added
  - ◊manufacturing labor is wages of people working on products

144

◊overhead includes all manufacturing costs that are not either raw materials or direct labor

•work in process flows into finished goods, then to cost of goods sold

---

Point of reference: Study Exhibit 7-3 in your text to review the difference in inventory flow between a manufacturer and a merchandiser.

How is cost of goods sold identified?

The **cost of goods sold equation** identifies those items sold:

Beginning inventory is merchandise or finished goods on hand when period begins

+ Purchases or transfers from work in process: more merchandise is purchased, or new items manufactured

= Goods available for sale: the total of the above two groups of items are all available to be sold to customers

- Ending inventory: not everything is sold; those items left unsold are ending inventory (and the following period's beginning inventory)

= Cost of goods sold: those items available, less any still on hand

Do you remember what gross profit (gross margin) is?

Gross profit equals sales less cost of goods sold

•reflects total markup on all goods sold during period

•expressed as a dollar amount or a **ratio (gross profit ÷ sales)**

How do inventory errors affect financial reporting?

Inventory equation—BI + P - EI = CGS—shows that inventory is key to the calculation of cost of goods sold

•if ending inventory is incorrect, balance sheet will be incorrectly reported, and cost of goods sold will be incorrect

•since one period's ending inventory automatically becomes next period's beginning inventory, that period, too, will have both an incorrect balance sheet and an incorrect income statement

•income statement effect would be the opposite in the two years, and thus by the end of the second year, retained earnings would be correct

145

•many errors are inadvertent, but it is also true that inventory fraud is one of the most common types of financial statement fraud

How is the cost of inventory determined?

In a situation where inventory costs have changed, and thus items are booked at different costs, it must be determined which items will be considered sold and which still in inventory

•four accepted methods exist for *allocating* goods available between ending inventory and cost of goods sold: these are *cost flow*, NOT physical flow, assumptions

◊**first-in, first-out** (**FIFO**): assumes that the oldest costs (first in) will be the first ones to be used for cost of goods sold (first out); thus most recent costs will remain in ending inventory

◊**last-in, first-out** (**LIFO**): costs of most recently acquired goods (last in) are used first for cost of goods sold (first out); thus, oldest costs become ending inventory

◊**weighted average** costing: total inventory cost + number of units available gives a weighted average cost per unit available; multiplied by units sold, or units in ending inventory

---

Point of reference: Carefully retrace the calculations in Exhibit 7-5, to be sure you understand the differences between these three methods of calculating inventory value and cost of goods sold.

◊**specific identification** requires the seller to know which precise items were sold; their cost is obtained from the accounting records and recorded as cost of goods sold

·only practical when inventory items are large, few in number, easily distinguishable one from the other, and/or very costly

•methods give different ending inventories, gross profits, net income

◊for example, when costs are rising, LIFO net income is lower; falling costs will produce higher net income

if inventory levels or costs drop, the effect will also be reversed

◊FIFO will have effects precisely the opposite of these

146

◊choice of method has reporting and tax considerations

•company may choose any method, regardless of physical flow of goods

•no requirement exists to use same method for all inventory

•inventory accounting must, however, be consistent from year to year

How does a company choose its inventory costing methods?

Costing method for reporting is chosen to reflect company's economic circumstances; tax method is chosen to pay as little tax, as late as possible

•**LIFO conformity rule** dictates that if LIFO is used for tax purposes, it must be used for reporting; for all other methods, the two can differ

◊LIFO tax saving (from lowered net income in times of inflation) is reversed if prices start to fall, or inventory is reduced

•for companies whose costs are dropping (high technology companies, for example) FIFO can be a better choice for tax purposes

How does the choice of available methods affect comparability?

In comparing companies, choice of inventory methods is not a problem, because companies must disclose inventory values using other methods than the one they report, if difference is material

•allows reader to convert statements from one method to another

•excess of FIFO over LIFO inventory known as **LIFO reserve**

◊difference in beginning inventory less difference in ending inventory equals difference in cost of goods sold

What is inventory turnover?

Inventory turnover measures the **liquidity** of inventory, that is, how close it is to becoming cash

•**turnover = cost of goods sold ÷ average inventory**

•note that if LIFO is used for inventories, the values can be greatly understated relative to cost of goods sold, making ratio distorted

◊best method is to use FIFO inventories and LIFO cost of goods sold: both are recent values

How does a LIFO liquidation affect reported values?

LIFO liquidation occurs when a LIFO company sells more inventory than it buys or produces

> •items from inventory have lower costs, so a higher gross profit results, and higher taxes
>
> •could be avoided by year-end inventory purchase
>
> •if a liquidation takes place, and effects are material, must be footnoted in financial statements, showing effect of liquidation, and income as if liquidation had not taken place

What is the lower of cost of market rule?

When goods in ending inventory can be replaced with identical goods at a lower cost, the lower cost should be used to value the inventory; called **LCM** or the **lower of cost or market** rule

> •rule also applies to damaged, obsolete, deteriorated items, which should be valued at net realizable value
>
> •rule reflects conservatism constraint
>
> •**replacement cost** is current purchase cost
>
> •**holding loss** is recognized in period in which cost dropped, not when item is sold
>
> > ◊net effect on combined current and future earnings is zero, since current cost of goods sold is reduced and future increased by the same amount; simply transfers loss to current period
>
> •recognition of a holding gain (if value of inventory actually increases) is not permitted
>
> •if **net realizable value** (sales price less selling costs) of an item drops below cost, difference is subtracted from inventory and added to cost of goods sold of the period of the adjustment

What is the difference between a periodic and a perpetual inventory system?

In a **periodic inventory system,** no up-to-date record of inventory is kept during the year

> •purchases of merchandise not recorded in inventory, but in a **purchases** account
>
> •count taken at the end of the period determines ending inventory, using one of the cost flow assumptions learned earlier in this chapter to value the items
>
> •ending inventory subtracted from goods available to determine cost of goods sold

•provides no inventory information during the period

•only justified in the past by its low cost and simplicity; the currently decreasing cost of computers negates this

A **perpetual inventory system** maintains constant records on the movement of inventory

•physical count still done periodically to confirm records and detect errors or theft

•purchases recorded directly to inventory

•the specific system used and how much detail is kept depend on company's needs

◊companies often need to keep track only of quantities, not costs

◊when costs are kept continuously, average cost or FIFO is usually used, seldom LIFO, which is more expensive and complex

What other factors are involved in the cost of goods purchased?

When purchased items are returned for any reason, an account called **purchase returns and allowances** is credited

•note the similarity to the seller's *sales returns and allowances*

Buyer also accounts for **purchase discounts** when paying within the early payment deadline

•purchase recorded at full cost; purchase discount account created when discount is actually taken at time of payment

◊see *sales discounts*, for seller, in Chapter 6

QUESTIONS AND EXERCISES

Multiple Choice:

Select the best answer for each question below, considering all the choices before you make your decision. Sometimes one answer will be *possible*, but another will be *better* .

1. In a manufacturing company, raw materials are

    a. items purchased as spare parts for their products.

    b. items intended for resale.

    c. items that will be used to manufacture the company's products.

    d. completed products that have not yet been sold.

    e. items ordered but not yet received.

2. A merchandiser's inventory consists of

    a. raw materials and finished goods.

    b. raw materials, work in process and finished goods.

    c. finished goods.

    d. merchandise inventory intended for resale.

    e. raw materials.

Use the following information, taken from the 1994 Annual Report of Wal-Mart Stores, Inc., and the cost of goods sold equation, to answer the next three questions:

	($ millions)		
	1994	1993	1992
ending inventory	11,483	9,780	7,857
cost of goods sold	53,444	44,175	34,786

3. What were 1994 purchases?

    a. 55,147

    b. 53,444

    c. 51,741

    d. 32,181

    e. 74,707

4. What is the beginning inventory for 1993?

    a. not given

    b. 7,857

    c. 11,483

    d. 9,780

    e. 34,395

5. Purchases for 1992 were 36,435. Calculate ending inventory for 1991.

    a. insufficient information is given

    b. 7,857

    c. 1,649

    d. 9,780

    e. 6,208

6. Fast Frank's Discounters adjusted their net income for 1994 by overstating ending inventory by $2 million. Ignoring taxes, if the incorrect number went undetected, retained earnings for 1994 would be _____ and retained earnings for 1995 would be _____

    a. overstated by $2 million; understated by $2 million

    b. overstated by $2 million; overstated by $2 million

    c. understated by $2 million; overstated by $2 million

    d. overstated by $2 million; unaffected

    e. understated by $2 million; understated by $2 million

Use the following information to answer the next 9 questions. Claemore Fruit and Sweet Shops order toffees by the pound. They made a number of purchases during July, at the following prices:

	pounds	cost per pound	total cost
beginning inventory	50	$1	$50
purchase, July 1	100	1.10	110
purchase, July 9	120	1.15	138
purchase, July 20	120	1.15	138
purchase, July 30	150	1.20	180

During this period, 480 pounds of toffees were sold at $1.45 per pound.

7. The weighted average cost of a pound of toffees was
   a. $1.12
   b. $1.11
   c. $1.14
   d. $11.95
   e. $1.15

8. Ending inventory under weighted average costing would be
   a. $60.00
   b. $68.40
   c. $72.00
   d. $547.20
   e. $540.00

9. If LIFO costing is used, the ending inventory will be
   a. $61
   b. $60
   c. $72
   d. $50
   e. $180

10. Under FIFO costing, the gross profit would be
    a. $544
    b. $696
    c. $152
    d. $555
    e. $141

11. The inventory costing method least likely to be used for this product is
    a. LIFO
    b. FIFO
    c. weighted average
    d. specific identification
    e. LCM

12. If the company's tax rate is 40%, using LIFO instead of FIFO could mean
    a. $6.60 increased taxes
    b. $6.60 taxes saved
    c. $4.40 taxes saved
    d. $4.40 increased taxes
    e. $11 taxes saved

13. A purchase of 100 pounds of toffees on July 31, at a cost of $1.25 per pound, would change FIFO cost of goods sold by _ and LIFO cost of goods sold by ____ .
    a. $0; $14.50 increase
    b. $14.50 increase; $0
    c. $0; $0
    d. $0; $14.50 decrease
    e. $14.50 decrease; $0

14. If this company uses LIFO for tax purposes in order to postpone payment of taxes as long as possible, then for reporting
    a. they are free to choose any inventory method they wish.
    b. they must disclose this fact.
    c. they must also use LIFO.
    d. they must use either LIFO or FIFO.
    e. they cannot use LIFO.

15. (Disregard question 13.) This company's LIFO reserve at the end of the period is
    a. $61
    b. $11
    c. $9.50
    d. $4.40
    e. $72

16. A LIFO liquidation occurs when

    a. a company converts from LIFO to FIFO.

    b. a company sells off all of its inventory.

    c. a company sells in one period more inventory than they purchase or manufacture.

    d. a company goes out of business.

    e. a company using LIFO experiences a decrease instead of an increase in merchandise cost.

17. The lower of cost or market rule (LCM) is applied

    a. when inventory costs less than it can be sold for.

    b. when the market value of long-lived assets is less than their cost.

    c. when inventory has been held for more than one year.

    d. at every year-end, to determine balance sheet values.

    e. when the replacement cost or net realizable value of inventory drops below the cost of the items.

18. In order to calculate cost of goods sold in a periodic inventory system, it is necessary to

    a. take a balance of the Merchandise Inventory account.

    b. add up sales receipts for the period.

    c. take a balance of the Cost of Goods Sold account.

    d. physically count the merchandise remaining in the inventory.

    e. subtract gross profit from sales.

19. A perpetual inventory system differs from a periodic system in that

    a. up-to-date inventory records are maintained.

    b. a uniform base stock of inventory is always kept on hand.

    c. the books of account are closed more often.

    d. a perpetual system regularly takes physical counts of inventory on hand.

    e. a periodic system breaks the year into measurable accounting periods.

20. The account Purchases is used

    a. in a perpetual system to record all purchases of inventory for resale.

    b. in a periodic system to record all purchases of inventory for resale.

    c. in both a perpetual and a periodic system to record all purchases of inventory for resale.

    d. only during the closing process.

    e. as a contra account to Inventory.

True or False?

For each of the following statements, place the letter "T" or "F" in the space before the statement to indicate whether you think the statement is true or false. Think about *why* each statement you mark with an "F" is false. Re-word each false statement to make it true.

_____ 21. The cost of goods sold equation states that beginning inventory + purchases + ending inventory = cost of goods sold.

_____ 22. The chief goals of inventory management are to have sufficient quantities of goods on hand to meet customer needs, while minimizing the costs of handling and storing those goods.

_____ 23. Work in process inventory for a merchandiser consists of items not yet displayed for sale.

_____ 24. Goods manufactured by a business, complete and ready for sale, are placed in merchandise inventory.

_____ 25. The materiality constraint sometimes allows a merchandiser to place "freight in" in an expense account, instead of inventorying it as part of the cost of merchandise.

_____ 26. An error in the measurement of ending inventory can affect the reported results of more than one year.

_____ 27. A company's choice of inventory costing method must at least approximate the physical flow of inventory.

_____ 28. The advantage of the specific identification method of inventory costing is that since items sold have to be individually identified, manipulation of results is very difficult.

_____ 29. The LIFO conformity rule requires that if LIFO is chosen for tax purposes, it must also be adopted for reporting.

_____ 30. The LIFO reserve can be used to convert reported financial results from LIFO to FIFO in order to compare the results of more than one company.

_____ 31. Even in a period of rising prices, a company that undergoes a LIFO liquidation could show higher net income than it would have under FIFO.

_____ 32. The lower of cost or market rule requires that damaged, deteriorated or obsolete items be marked down to a cost that will allow a reasonable profit when they are sold.

_____ 33. The replacement cost of an item is the current purchase price of the latest model of that item.

A Few Words from You ...

Discuss each of the following questions briefly. Show calculations where appropriate.

34. **How does inventory affect the cash-to-cash cycle?** Refer to Chapter 3, and review the concept of the operating, or cash-to-cash, cycle. Given what you have now learned in this current chapter on inventory flows, discuss the differences in the operating cycle for a merchandiser and a manufacturer. How will this affect the cash needs of each type of company? Why is this important to outside users of the companies' financial statements?

35. **Inventory profits?** Vera Sure has been the manager for five years of the poster division of Familiar Faces, a company that buys posters and T-shirts with celebrity portraits on them from printers and offers them for sale in shops near college campuses. She has always believed that her main job is to keep the customer happy, and that part of that involves not being "out of stock" on an item that someone wants. Vera regularly stocked extra inventory to meet unexpected demands. Vera was promoted on January 1, 1995, to manage the company's discount outlet in Maine, and her old position in the poster division was given to Justin Time. Justin had recently earned an MBA, and was full of new management ideas. He was particularly interested in what he had read about controlling the size of inventories to keep carrying costs down. He decided that the poster division had far too much extra inventory, and wanted to reduce it significantly. This would both save the company money, and enhance profits.

Figure 1 shows abbreviated income statements for Vera's five-year tenure, and a partial statement for Justin's first year. Justin is very pleased with his results. He thinks that the numbers prove he was right, and that profits are going to keep growing under his new policy.

Figure 1

Familiar Faces
Comparative Income Statements
for the years 1990 through 1995

	1990 #	1990 $	1991 #	1991 $	1992 #	1992 $	1993 #	1993 $	1994 #	1994 $	1995 #	1995 $
S	1000	5000	1100	6600	1300	9100	1500	12000	1800	16200	2000	20000
BI	100	200	200	450	250	600	300	775	400	1175	500	
+ P	1100	2750	1150	3450	1350	4725	1600	6400	1900	8550		
- EI	200	450	250	600	300	775	400	1175	500	1625	200	
= C/S	1000	2500	1100	3300	1300	4550	1500	6000	1800	8100		
GP	-	2500	-	3300	-	4550	-	6000	-	8100	-	
OE	-	2000	-	2200	-	2600	-	3000	-	3600	-	4000
NI	-	500	-	1100	-	1950	-	3000	-	4500	-	

\# = number of posters

$ = sales or cost dollars (unit sales or cost * number of units)

a. Which inventory costing method is Familiar Faces using? Explain why you think so.
What is their markup policy? Which number in the financial statements tells you this?

b. Using your conclusion from (a), complete the information for 1995, Justin's first year.

c. Which figure in Justin's income statement might cause questions from an alert analyst?
Why? Explain Justin's results. Can Justin expect profits to continue to grow in the same
proportion?

d. Is Justin's goal—to reduce inventories—a good one?

e. Do your answers to (c) and (d) contradict one another? Explain.

36. **What effect does the LIFO reserve have?** The following figures were selected from the 1993 Annual Report of the General Electric Company (GE):

	1993	1992
Cost of goods sold	22,606	
Income from continuing operations	6,575	
Inventory on LIFO basis	3,824	4,574
LIFO reserve	1,629	1,808

a. What would inventory be on a FIFO basis in each of the two years (1992 and 1993)?

b. What is the difference in 1993 cost of goods sold and income from continuing operations between the reported LIFO basis and if FIFO had been used?

c. Calculate GE's inventory turnover using the cost of goods sold and inventory figures reported in the financial statements. Now, recalculate it using the FIFO inventory figures. Is the difference material? Explain which calculation you would prefer to use to judge liquidity of the company and why.

37. **Is LCM an ethical question?** When a company adjusts an inventory account to the lower of cost or market, because of a decline in the net realizable value of those inventory items, to what accounts do the debit and credit parts of that journal entry go? Might the company have an incentive *not* to make this entry? Why? What incentive is there for the company to comply with accepted practice?

Team up!

Get together in teams of 3 - 5 members to decide each of the following:

38. **Can you find the missing information?** The following information is taken from the 1993 Annual Report of Nike, Inc. for 1993. Fill in the blanks. Before you begin, look over the information given. Which two basic formulas are you going to use?

($millions)

	1993	1992	1991	1990	1989	1988
Revenues	3931	3405	?	2235	1711	1203
Cost of goods sold	?	?	1851	834	?	?
Gross profit	1544	1316	1153	?	?	400
End inventory	593	?	587	309	223	198
Purchases	?	1941	?	?	1100	---

39. **What is gross profit?** Using the information from this and the previous chapter, how many different things can you list that a company can do that will affect its gross profit, either as a dollar amount or as a ratio (%)?

Is this ratio subject to manipulation? What can you as a reader of the information do to assure yourself of the reliability of the figure you are seeing?

40. **Is there enough information here?** The following table contains alternative ending inventory figures for a company that began business on January 1, 1995. They are trying to decide which inventory method to use. Use the information to answer the questions following.

	FIFO	LIFO	Weighted Average
December 31, 1995	20	100	71
December 31, 1996	150	130	120

Were inventory prices rising or falling during 1995?

During 1995, which inventory method will produce the highest net income?

Which method will produce the lowest net income?

Which method would the company choose in 1995 if tax savings are their primary consideration? Would they still consider this a good choice in 1996?

Which method gives the highest net income in 1996?

Which gives the lowest net income in 1996?

Which method gives the most realistic balance sheet inventory value?

Which method shows the most realistic income statement value?

And just for the fun of it ...

Abbreviations!! By this point in the course, you must be convinced that nobody spells out anything in business when they can think of a catchy acronym or initials instead. Check your "initial IQ" by going through the following list of definitions of commonly seen abbreviations and writing down as many of the abbreviations as you can.

_____ a. Measurement rules used to develop information for published financial statements.

_____ b. The professional organization that certifies public accountants and regulates professional conduct.

_____ c. The private sector body with the primary responsibility for working out detailed rules for financial reporting.

_____ d. An inventory cost flow assumption that assumes that the most recent prices are given to ending inventory.

162

_____ e. The form on which a company submits annual financial data to the Securities and Exchange Commission.

_____ f. An accountant who has fulfilled professional requirements necessary to qualify to give a formal opinion on the fairness of a company's financial data.

_____ g. The cost of the merchandise that the customer just bought.

_____ h. The top officer in a company.

_____ i. Left side.

_____ j. An inventory cost flow assumption that assumes that the most recent costs go to cost of goods sold first.

_____ k. The government body that sets reporting regulations for publicly held companies.

_____ l. The top accounting officer in a company.

_____ m. A professionally certified accountant working in private industry.

_____ n. The rule requiring a company to reduce the valuation of obsolete inventory.

_____ o. Right side.

SOLUTIONS

Multiple choice:
1. (c) 2. (d) 3. (a) 4. (b) 5. (e) 6. (d) 7. (c) 8. (b) 9. (a) 10. (c) 11. (d) 12. (c) 13. (a) 14. (c) 15. (b) 16. (c) 17. (e) 18. (d) 19. (a) 20. (b)

True or false:
21. False. The equation is: beginning inventory + purchases - ending inventory = cost of goods sold.

22. True.

23. False. Work in process is a *manufacturer's* inventory of items not yet completed.

24. False. Goods completed by a manufacturer are placed in Finished Goods inventory.

25. True.

26. True.

27. False. The inventory costing method is a cost flow method, and need not have anything to do with physical flow.

28. False. Specific identification lends itself to its own form of manipulation. A company could select certain items to sell first, over other identical items, because of their cost.

29. True.

30. True.

31. True.

32. False. The LCM rule requires that damaged, obsolete or deteriorated goods be marked down to their current cost or net realizable value, leaving no "cushion" for future profit.

33. False. The replacement cost is the current cost of an identical item.

A few words from you:

35. a. The inventory method used is LIFO.
b.

	1995	
	#	$
S	2000	20,000
BI	500	1625
+ P	1700	8500
- EI	200	450
= CGS	2000	9675
GP	-	10,325
OE	-	4000
NI	-	6325

36.   a. 1992 inventory = 4574 + 1808 = 6382; 1993 inventory = 3824 + 1629 = 5453

   b.   difference in beginning inventory   1808
              - difference in ending inventory   1629
          = difference in cost of goods sold   179

c. turnover = cost of goods sold ÷ average inventory

$$= 22606 \div [(4574 + 3824) / 2]$$

$$= 5.4$$

alternatively, turnover = $22606 \div ((6382 + 5453) / 2) = 3.8$

38.

	($millions)					
	1993	1992	1991	1990	1989	1988
Revenues	3931	3405	3004	2235	1711	1203
Cost of goods sold	2387	2089	1851	834	1075	803
Gross profit	1544	1316	1153	1401	636	400
End inventory	593	439	587	309	223	198
Purchases	2541	1941	2129	920	1100	---

And just for the fun of it:

a. GAAP

b. AICPA

c. FASB

d. FIFO

e. 10-K

f. CPA

g. CGS

h. CEO

i. Dr

j. LIFO

k. SEC

l. CFO

m. CMA

n. LCM

o. Cr

CHAPTER 8

OPERATIONAL ASSETS— PROPERTY, PLANT, AND EQUIPMENT; NATURAL RESOURCES; AND INTANGIBLES

The time to repair the roof is when the sun is shining.
John F. Kennedy

OVERVIEW

In previous chapters, we discussed the current assets of a business. These assets are critical for the operations of a business but many of them do not directly produce value. A business could not survive without cash, but cash does not produce goods or services that can be sold to customers. In this chapter, we will discuss noncurrent assets that are sometimes called productive assets. Many of the noncurrent assets produce value such as a factory that manufactures cars. These assets present some interesting accounting problems because they benefit a number of accounting periods.

LEARNING OBJECTIVES

1. Define, classify, and explain the nature of operational assets.

2. Apply the cost principle to measure and record operational assets.

3. Apply the matching principle to record and report depreciation.

4. Describe the financial statement impact of a change in depreciation estimates.

5. Account for ordinary and extraordinary repairs.

6. Record the disposal of operational assets.

7. Account for natural resources and intangible assets, including amortization.

CHAPTER OUTLINE

What are operational assets?

Operational assets are those assets used to produce goods or services for sale
- **tangible** assets have physical substance; usually called property, plant, and equipment
    - ◊**land** is not depreciated
    - ◊**buildings, fixtures and equipment** are depreciated
    - ◊**natural resources** are extracted from nature
- **intangible** assets are *rights*, with no physical substance

How is the cost of an asset determined?

The **acquisition cost** of an asset includes all reasonable and necessary costs to acquire it, place it in its operational location, and prepare it for use
- financing costs are not reported as cost of asset, but are recorded as interest expense
- cost includes current market value of any non-cash considerations
- repairs to put the asset in operational condition are included in asset account, but repairs incurred after asset is in service are expensed
- if company constructs the asset itself, interest incurred while asset is under construction is included in cost: **capitalized interest**

A **basket purchase** occurs when several assets are acquired for one lump sum
- cost of each asset must be measured and recorded separately, and purchase price apportioned between them
    - ◊relative market value is a logical basis for this apportionment

How is the cost of an asset allocated to the periods in which it is used?

The cost of an asset is allocated over its life, except in the case of land, whose cost normally remains an asset until the land is sold or modified
- **depreciation** is the allocation of the cost of tangible assets
    - ◊**contra asset** account, accumulated depreciation, is used for the credit
- **depletion** is the allocation of the cost of natural resources
    - ◊contra account may or may not be used for credit
- **amortization** is the term given to the allocation of the cost of an intangible asset

167

◊may or may not use a contra asset for credit

•in all cases, operating expense is recorded

•balance sheet amount—cost less accumulated depreciation—is the **book value** of the asset

How is depreciation calculated?

It is necessary to know acquisition cost, estimated residual value, and estimated expected life

•**residual value** is the amount expected to be recovered when the asset is disposed of at the end of its useful life

•**estimated useful life** is economic life to present owner

◊determined under **continuity assumption**: business will continue to operate indefinitely

A number of depreciation *methods* are acceptable

•**straight line depreciation** assumes an equal part of the asset's usefulness expires each year of its life; depreciation expense =

$$\frac{\text{cost - residual value}}{\text{life in years}}$$

•**units of production** is similar to straight line, but allocates cost based on periodic output of asset rather than the passage of time; depreciation expense =

$$\frac{\text{cost - residual value}}{\text{life in units of production}}$$

◊necessary to measure output each period in order to determine proper amount of expense

◊depreciation varies with production or use of the asset

•if an asset is more efficient or productive in its early years, or repair costs increase as time goes on, company may want to charge more depreciation in earlier years, and less in later years; an **accelerated depreciation** method is used

◊not often used for reporting

◊two methods most frequently used are **sum-of-the-years'-digits** and **declining balance**

·**sum-of-the-years' digits** multiplies cost less residual by a fraction:

∞numerator is the specific year of life, in inverse order

∞denominator is sum of the years of life of the asset (which may be calculated by the formula, **n [(n+1)÷2]** where n is the years of life)

∞thus, (cost - residual) * (years of life remaining ÷ sum of years of life) = expense

∞amount of depreciation starts out higher than straight line, and declines as life of asset goes on

·**declining balance** applies an *acceleration rate* to the straight line rate; for example, double declining balance would be 200% of the straight line rate, *applied to the net book value* of the asset each year

∞rate cannot exceed 200%

For tax purposes, a separate set of records is needed, because the objectives of GAAP and the Internal Revenue Service are different, so both require individual depreciation methods

•the objective of reporting is to provide financial information, useful in predicting future cash flows

•objective of the Revenue Code is to raise revenue to support the federal government

◊**MACRS**, or Modified Accelerated Cost Recovery System, is similar to declining balance

·uses very short asset lives, not matched to economic life of asset to the company

·meant to encourage investment in productive assets by reducing cash paid out for taxes

Partial year depreciation usually a matter of company policy, such as

•half year in year acquired

•full year for assets acquired before July 1, none for those after July 1

•full month for assets acquired before 15th, none for those after 15th

Can the estimates made to calculate depreciation expense be revised?

If experience with the asset shows that one or both of the estimates—the life of the asset and the residual value—should be revised, it is done prospectively, that is, from the point of revision forward

•expense for remainder of life will be based on current net book value and new estimate(s)

•no changes are made to past figures, since they were based on best estimates at the time

•in conformity with **comparability concept**, only done when new estimate better measures the periodic income of the business

How does depreciation affect cash flow?

Cash flow occurs when asset is acquired; depreciation expense involves no cash, nor is depreciation a source of cash

> •however, depreciation policy for tax purposes can affect amount of cash paid out for taxes, or conserved

How are repairs, maintenance and additions to assets accounted for?

An **expenditure** is the payment of money for goods or services; an **expense** is an expenditure that benefits only the current period

> •for an asset, expenditures are classified as capital expenditures or revenue expenditures

>> ·a **revenue expenditure** benefits only one period and is expensed

>>> ∞**ordinary repairs and maintenance** keep the asset in its usual operating condition, and are expensed

>> ·a **capital expenditure** benefits more than one accounting period and is added to cost of asset and depreciated

>>> ∞**extraordinary repairs** increase the efficiency or the life of the asset and are **capitalized**, or debited to the related asset account

>>> ∞**additions** are extensions or enlargements of an asset; added to asset account and depreciated over life of asset or life of addition, whichever is shorter

>> ·sometimes deciding whether an expenditure should be capitalized or expensed is a matter of judgment; materiality is often a company's criterion for this decision

How is the disposal of an asset recorded?

Business need not hold an asset for its entire anticipated life; may dispose of an asset that is no longer needed, or may want a newer asset, or the asset may be lost or destroyed

> •remove asset (with a credit)
> •remove the related accumulated depreciation (with a debit) from the books of account
> •record any cash or other assets received (debit)

•the difference between net book value and receipts is gain (credit) or loss (debit) on disposal

◊not a revenue or expense, because this is a "non-operating" item

What is different about the accounting for natural resources?

A **natural resource**, or wasting asset, is an asset that occurs in nature, and is removed, or depleted

•extracting natural resources has a significant effect on the environment, and thus the companies that do so receive a lot of attention

•the process of periodic extraction is known as depletion

◊depletion rate = total acquisition and development cost ÷ estimated units of resource that will be obtained

·same procedure as units of production

What are intangible assets, and how are they accounted for?

An **intangible asset** is valuable because of rights or privileges granted to the asset's owner by law

•recorded at cost only if purchased; if the asset is developed internally, development costs normally expensed

•after acquisition, intangible assets are amortized over their *legal* or *economic lives*, whichever is shorter

◊**patents** are the inventors' rights to products or processes

·typically have a 17-year legal life

·amortization debited to expense and typically credited to asset, not a contra account

◊**copyrights** are rights to written work—music, art, literary

·legal life expire 50 years after the author's death

·accounted for similarly to patents

◊**franchises** and **licenses** are granted by the government or a private organization for a specific time and purpose

·franchises are contracts, between *franchisor* (grantor) and *franchisee* (grantee)

◊**leaseholds** are contracts granting the right to use a specifically named asset or assets

·if the lessee makes improvements to the leased property, they are known as **leasehold improvements** and recorded as assets

∞amortized over the life of the improvements or the lease, whichever is shorter

◊**trademarks** are names, images or slogans associated with a company or product

·development costs are expensed

·no costs recorded unless they are purchased

◊**goodwill** is the favorable reputation a company has earned

·internally generated goodwill cannot be recorded

·can only be recorded if the company is purchased; then, goodwill is the cost in excess of the fair market value of the purchased company's net assets (assets less liabilities)

·amortized over a period not to exceed 40 years; credit is usually directly to the asset, not a contra account

SUPPLEMENT A
TRADING IN ASSETS

How is a purchase recorded when an old asset is traded in for a new one?

Typically, an old asset plus cash are exchanged for a new asset

•if assets are similar and no cash is paid, asset acquired is recorded at book value of asset traded in

•if assets are dissimilar and no cash is paid, asset acquired is recorded at estimated market value of asset traded in

•if assets are similar and cash is exchanged along with old asset, asset acquired is recorded at book value of the old asset plus the cash paid

•if dissimilar assets are exchanged and cash is paid in addition to old asset, asset acquired is recorded at the estimated market value of the old asset plus the cash paid, but not in excess of the market value of the asset acquired

QUESTIONS AND EXERCISES

Multiple Choice:

Consider all the answers to the following questions, and circle the letter of the one that best answers the question. If more than one answer is possible, choose the one that is *best*..

1. _____ assets have physical substance, whereas _____ assets have no physical substance, but rather grant rights to their owner.
   a. operational; long-lived
   b. tangible; intangible
   c. operational; non-operating
   d. intangible; tangible
   e. tangible; natural resources

2. Financing charges (interest) associated with the purchase of an asset are
   a. always expensed in the period in which they are incurred.
   b. always included in the cost of the asset.
   c. normally expensed when an asset is purchased; but if the company constructs an asset for its own use the interest incurred while the asset is under construction is included in the cost of the asset.
   d. expensed in total when the asset is purchased, and capitalized in total when the company builds the asset itself.
   e. may be expensed or capitalized at the discretion of the company.

3. When a basket purchase takes place
   a. the assets are recorded as a single asset, at the purchase cost.
   b. the assets are recorded individually at their market values.
   c. the assets are recorded as a single asset at the total of their market values.
   d. each individual asset is recorded separately, at an apportioned cost based on the relative market values of all the assets purchased.
   e. each individual asset is recorded separately, with the cost evenly divided between them.

4. The primary purpose of depreciation is

    a. to allocate the cost of an asset over its useful life in conformity with the matching principle.

    b. to determine the market value of an asset at any point of its life.

    c. to delay as long as possible the payment of taxes by charging expense against income.

    d. to approximate the total cost of using an asset.

    e. to decrease the value of an asset in conformity with the conservatism principle.

5. Residual value is

    a. the difference at any point in time between net book value and market value.

    b. the excess of cost over accumulated depreciation.

    c. the part of the acquisition cost of an asset expected to be recovered when the asset is disposed of at the end of its usefulness to the current owner.

    d. the part of an asset not yet depreciated at any point in time.

    e. the scrap value of the asset.

Use the following information to answer the next 9 questions:

You have become familiar with Delta Airlines through your text. One of their competitors is American Airlines (AMR Corporation). At the end of fiscal year 1992, American had some $13,194 million in property and equipment on their balance sheet, net of accumulated depreciation. Their non-flight equipment, worth just under $2,500 million, is depreciated by the straight-line method over average lives of from 3 to 15 years. We will use as an example a hypothetical piece of ground service equipment, purchased at the beginning of a year for $9,000. The equipment is expected to be used for 5 years, after which it will have a residual value of $750. Consider some comparisons under varying depreciation assumptions:

6. Under the straight-line method, the second year's depreciation expense will be
    _____, and the remaining net book value _____ .

    a. $5,700; $1,650

    b. $1,650; $4,950

    c. $4,950; $1,650

    d. $1,650; $3,300

    e. $1,650; $5,700

7. At the end of the asset's usefulness to American, it will have a net book value
   a. of $9,000.
   b. of $8,250.
   c. of $750.
   d. of $0.
   e. equal to its market value.

8. Had American used sum-of-the-years' digits depreciation instead, the second year's depreciation would have been _____ and the ending net book value that year _____.
   a. $2,200; 4,950
   b. $1,100; $6,600
   c. $2,200; $3,300
   d. $2,200; $4,050
   e. $4,050; $2,200

9. Sum-of-the-years' digits, along with the _____ method, are known as an accelerated depreciation methods.
   a. straight-line
   b. declining-balance
   c. units-of-production
   d. depletion
   e. annuity

10. Under double-declining-balance depreciation, American would record _____ depreciation expense in Year 1 of this asset's life, leaving a net book value of _____

   a. $3,600; $5,400
   b. $5,400; $3,600
   c. $3,300; $5,700
   d. $3,300; $4,950
   e. $5,700; $3,300

11. If declining-balance depreciation is used throughout the life of this asset, the net book value at the end of year 5 should be

    a. $416
    b. $700
    c. $750
    d. $0
    e. $466

12. For tax purposes, American probably uses the _____ method to calculate depreciation.

    a. Modified Accelerated Cost Recovery System
    b. straight-line
    c. sum-of-the-years' digits
    d. 200% declining balance
    e. units of service

13. Now assume that at the beginning of the fourth year of this asset's life, using straight-line depreciation, when the asset has a net book value of _____ , American decides that they will actually be able to use the asset for eight (8) years, instead of five. At the end of that time it will have no residual value. Depreciation expense for each of the remaining years of life, beginning with year 4, if American uses the straight-line method, will be

_____ .

    a. $4,050; $1,650
    b. $4,050; $810
    c. $3,300; $660
    d. $5,907; $1,031
    e. $4,050; $1,125

14. If American completely rebuilt a motor on this piece of equipment after four years, extending the life of the equipment three years beyond the original estimate of useful life and increasing the residual value to $1,000, this would be classified as a _____ expenditure, and the money spent for the rebuild would be _____ .

    a. capital expenditure; capitalized as a separate asset

    b. capital expenditure; capitalized as part of the cost of the equipment

    c. revenue expenditure; capitalized as part of the cost of the equipment

    d. revenue expenditure; expensed in the period in which it was spent

    e. capital expenditure; expensed in the period in which it was spent

15. Pi Products had some surplus office furniture that had an original cost of $60,000 and accumulated depreciation of $48,000. They sold the entire lot of this furniture to Iota Inc. for $20,000 cash. The journal entry to record this transaction would be:

a.

Cash	20,000	
Cost of sales	60,000	
Sales		20,000
Furniture		60,000

b.

Cash	20,000	
Furniture		12,000
Gain on disposal of furniture		8,000

c.

Cash	20,000	
Accumulated depreciation, furniture	48,000	
Furniture		60,000
Gain on disposal of furniture		8,000

d.

Cost of goods sold	12,000	
Cash	20,000	
Sales		20,000
Gain on disposal of furniture		12,000

e.

Cash	20,000	
Accumulated depreciation, furniture	48,000	
Furniture		60,000
Sales		8,000

16. Depletion is the term used to describe the periodic cost allocation process over the life of

    a. an intangible asset.

    b. land.

    c. a building.

    d. supplies.

    e. a natural resource.

17. All of the following are intangible assets except

    a. a copyright.

    b. a McDonald's franchise.

    c. goodwill.

    d. an offshore oil well.

    e. a leasehold on a large office building.

Use the following information for the next three questions:

Shrewsbury Company owned a building that had originally cost $45,000, and had accumulated depreciation of $28,000. The building had a current estimated market value of $60,000. Shrewsbury exchanged this building for land with a market value of $70,000.

18. In addition to the building, Shrewsbury gave the owner of the land $5,000 cash. The land would be recorded on the books of Shrewsbury Company at a value of

    a. $70,000.

    b. $65,000.

    c. $60,000.

    d. $17,000.

    e. $22,000.

19. Had the exchange taken place as stated, with a $5,000 cash payment, but the asset traded in was another plot of land instead of a building, then the new land would be recorded at

    a. $70,000.

    b. $65,000.

    c. $22,000.

    d. $17,000.

    e. $60,000.

20. Review question 18. If the cash paid had been $20,000 instead of $5,000, and a building exchanged for the land, the value at which the new land was recorded would have been

    a. $70,000.

    b. $80,000.

    c. $37,000.

    d. $17,000.

    e. $60,000.

True or False?

For each of the following statements, place the letter "T" or "F" in the space before the statement to indicate whether you think the statement is true or false. Think about *why* each statement you mark with an "F" is false. Be sure that you understand the concepts: re-word each false statement to make it true.

_____ 21. The cost of an asset includes all reasonable and necessary costs to acquire the asset, put it in place, and prepare it for its intended use.

_____ 22. Any non-cash assets exchanged in the purchase of an asset cannot be included in the capitalized cost of the new asset because their value is uncertain.

_____ 23. Interest is never included in the capitalized cost of an asset; it is always a period expense.

_____ 24. Amortization and depletion are procedurally similar to depreciation, except that they are associated with different types of assets.

_____ 25. Depreciation expense is an estimate, because two of the amounts it is based on are estimated amounts.

_____ 26. The useful life assigned to a tangible asset is the number of years that asset could be expected to last under normal use for the average user.

_____ 27. A change in the estimate of either useful life or residual value violates the comparability concept and is therefore discouraged and rarely done.

_____ 28. A company wishing to improve its cash flow should change for reporting purposes from the straight-line method to an accelerated method of depreciation.

_____ 29. An extraordinary repair is one that occurs infrequently, is very costly, and increases the useful life or efficiency of the asset involved.

_____ 30. Sometimes the decision about whether money spent on an asset is a revenue expenditure or a capital expenditure will be made based on materiality.

_____ 31. Natural resources are often called wasting assets because they render the area around them useless for the future after they are removed.

_____ 32. Goodwill can only be acquired when a company is purchased.

A Few Words from You ...

For each of the following, briefly discuss the pertinent issues involved. Support your answers with calculations where required.

33. **How do they compare?** A good way to understand the differences in annual expense between the various depreciation methods is to prepare a chart comparing expense and net book value annually throughout the life of a single asset. We will assume that a company purchases an asset for $47,000; they assign it a 6-year life, with an expected residual value of $5,000. Complete the chart below, filling in each year's depreciation expense under straight-line, sum-of-the-year's digits, and double (200%) declining balance depreciation. Also fill in the net book value of the asset at the end of each year.

	STRAIGHT LINE		SUM-OF- YEARS' DIGITS		DECLINING BALANCE	
YEAR	DEPR. EXP.	END NBV	DEPR. EXP.	END NBV	DEPR. EXP.	END. NBV
PURCHASE	-		-		-	
1						
2						
3						
4						
5						
6						
TOTAL		N/A		N/A		N/A

Answer the following based on your completed chart:

a. Which method produces the highest total depreciation expense? Explain your answer to someone who does not understand the concept of depreciation.

b. Which is the most accelerated method? When might a company want to use this method?

c. Which method, based on your reading of the chapter, is the most popularly used? Why do you think this is true?

d. Besides the mathematical procedure, what characteristics of the double-declining-balance method differ from the other methods? Explain why.

e. Which method most closely resembles the method prescribed by the IRS for use on corporate income tax reporting? What is the chief difference that makes the tax method unsuitable for reporting to stockholders?

34. **Can we put a value on this?** You started your own company two years ago, publishing a magazine that gives students a guide to the sights, sounds, snacks and shopping in the area of their college campuses. After two successful years of operating out of a rented office, you have an opportunity to buy a very small retail building, on a convenient back street near the campus of one of the major schools in your customer base. The owner has agreed on a price of $165,000 plus a five percent interest in your growing company for the land, building, and all the furnishings in the building. The former tenant was a small retail establishment that went south and left many furnishings behind. You can probably sell off some of the store fixtures, but the office furniture and an older but working computer will be useful to you, so you will keep those.

How are you going to record this purchase on your books of account? Describe in practical terms how you would go about determining a value or the individual components of this transaction, and how it should be recorded (you do not have to actually calculate specific amounts) in your company's books of account.

35. **Space in the sky?** AMR Corporation (American Airlines) had the following footnote in their 1992 Annual Report:

> *Route Acquisition Costs*   Route acquisition costs, aggregating $1.2 billion at December 31, 1992, net of accumulated amortization of $66 million, represent the purchase price attributable to routes acquired and are being amortized on a straight-line basis over 40 years.

What kind of asset is a "route?" Explain why.

What is the average age of this asset? Show calculations to support your answer. Is the age of this asset of the same importance as the age of, say, an airplane? Why or why not? Do you think this might have anything to do with the life over which this asset is amortized? Explain.

36. **Why not take some profits?** You have been told that a company sets a residual value on an asset in the amount that they expect to recover from the sale of that asset when its useful life to them is over. Explain, citing the appropriate accounting principle(s) or constraint(s), why a company would not deliberately keep this amount low in order to guarantee a modest profit when the asset is sold.

Team up!

Work on the following projects in teams of 3–5 members. Divide up the work and share your abilities.

37. **Are you sure you want to buy this?** Refresh you memory on the sections of this chapter that discuss the elements of the cost of an asset, and the difference between capital and revenue expenditures. Research the purchase of a major item that you yourself (or someone else in your group) might at some time consider buying. Choose something fairly complex, like a car, a set of furnishings for a room, a boat, or, if you want to get really ambitious, a house. Make some calls, or visits, to the appropriate retailers, banks, to find out what is involved in the purchase. List as many items as you can find that you will have to spend money on in order to buy this asset and put it into service. Is your asset going to be new or used? What difference will this make? Of the expenditures you will have to make, will all of them be includable in the capitalized cost of the asset, or are some expenses?

38. **To capitalize or not to capitalize … ?** Consider the following list of expenditures that a company might make. For each one, indicate whether it would be considered a capital or a revenue expenditure. There might be a couple that do not fit either category, at least immediately. Explain what would be done with them. For each item, would any of the following affect your answer? Explain.

     •the size of the hypothetical company
     •whether the company is buying one, or more than one, of the item in this purchase
     •the intended use of the item

a. a building

b. 500 packages of copier paper

c. an electric stapler

d. replacement of a cracked engine block on a company truck that has been driven for 35,000 miles

e. replacement of a cracked engine block on a company truck that has been driven for 185,000 miles

f. an office chair

g. an ink-jet printer for a computer

h. a one-time fee for the right to use a copyrighted trade name on products

i. a liquor license for a restaurant

j. potted plants for a building lobby

39. **How does MACRS work?** Call your local IRS office (they're in the government "blue pages" of your telephone book) and ask them to send you information on the Modified Accelerated Cost Recovery System. Explain briefly how MACRS works.

Go back to the chart you prepared for question 33 in this chapter of your Study Guide. Add two columns to the chart for MACRS and fill in the correct numbers. Assume the asset purchased is computer equipment.

Explain why these two columns are so different from the other methods of calculating depreciation.

If this company pays taxes at a rate of about 40%, how much will they save in the first year by using MACRS rather than straight line? What will be the difference if MACRS is compared to the other methods?

Prepare a chart that will show the book / tax difference between straight-line and MACRS for each year of the asset's life, and how the two methods will compare in total. Explain your results and the purpose of the tax method to someone who does not understand the difference.

And just for the fun of it ...

Assets come in a lot of sizes, and are paid for in many ways. One giant asset of current interest is the one being constructed in Atlanta, Georgia, for the 1996 Summer Olympics. Actually, it is a number of assets. The $1.6 billion budget includes about $470 million for construction of athletic facilities, and $47 million for the Olympic village. How do you think they will pay for all this? What happens when the Olympics are over? You have listened to all the news, but have you thought about it in business terms? Do ticket sales cover it all? Is this some sort of charity? Whose?

SOLUTIONS

Multiple choice:

1. (b) 2. (c) 3. (d) 4. (a) 5. (c) 6. (e) 7. (c) 8. (d) 9. (b) 10. (a) 11. (c) 12. (a) 13. (b) 14. (b) 15. (c) 16. (e) 17. (d) 18. (b) 19. (c) 20. (a)

True or false:

21. True.

22. False. When non-cash assets are involved, they are valued at their fair market value if determinable, or the exchange is valued at the fair market value of the asset purchased.

23. False. Interest during construction may be included if the asset is constructed by the company.

24. True.

25. True.

26. False. The useful life is the length of time the purchasing company intends to use the asset, regardless of its potential economic life.

27. False. The comparability concept is certainly violated here, but in the interest of more accurate matching of use of an asset to revenues generated. If this is the case, the change is justified and allowable.

28. False. Depreciation method does not affect cash flow, except in the sense that it can save taxes in the early years of an asset's life. Since depreciation is a non-cash expense, no cash enters or leaves the company.

29. True.

30. True.

31. False. Hopefully, the area can and will be reclaimed after extraction. They are called wasting assets because they are physically diminished by their extraction, until there is theoretically none of the asset left.

32. True.

A few words from you...

33.

	STRAIGHT LINE		SUM-OF- YEARS' DIGITS		DECLINING BALANCE	
YEAR	DEPR. EXP.	END NBV	DEPR. EXP.	END NBV	DEPR. EXP.	END. NBV
PURCHASE	-	47,000	-	47,000	-	47,000
1	7,000	40,000	12,000	35,000	15,510	31,490
2	7,000	33,000	10,000	25,000	10,392	21,098
3	7,000	26,000	8,000	17,000	6,962	14,136
4	7,000	19,000	6,000	11,000	4,665	9,471
5	7,000	12,000	4,000	7,000	3,125	6,346
6	7,000	5,000	2,000	5,000	1,346	5,000*
TOTAL	42,000	N/A	42,000	N/A	42,000	N/A

*The final year's depreciation expense had to be reduced from the calculated 2,094 to the 1,346 above in order not to depreciate the asset below its residual value. Calculations were performed using two decimal places in the multiplier. Your answer may vary somewhat depending upon how many decimals you use.

And just for the fun of it ...

Some Olympic facts, which will hopefully fuel your thinking and make you want to look for more:

•Organizers think tickets will bring in about $261 million dollars if they sell, as expected, 62% of the 11 million tickets available. Average ticket price: $40. Tickets to opening ceremonies can run as high as $600.

•Corporate sponsorship will be a big factor in paying for the Olympics, as well as television rights both in the United States and around the world.

•A novel idea is likely to be more productive than its originators ever dreamed. They will sell individually engraved bricks to line the pathway through the 70-acre Olympic Park. For $35 you can have a brick engraved with your name. Bricks of family members can be arranged together. These will be marketed by Atlanta-based Home Depot (see Chapter 14 in your text).

CHAPTER 9

MEASURING AND REPORTING LIABILITIES

God gave us two eyes so we can keep one on the money supply and the other on interest rates.

Paul A. Samuelson

OVERVIEW

In the previous chapters, we discussed business and accounting issues related to the assets held by a company. In this chapter and the next two, we will shift our focus to the other side of the balance sheet to see how managers finance the operations of their business and the acquisition of productive assets. We will discuss various types of liabilities in Chapters 9 and 10 and examine owners' equity in Chapter 11.

LEARNING OBJECTIVES

1. Define and classify liabilities.

2. Record and report current liabilities.

3. Compare current and long-term liabilities.

4. Apply deferred income tax allocation.

5. Explain liabilities for retirement benefits.

6. Record and report contingent liabilities.

7. Apply the concepts of future and present values of a single amount.

8. Apply present value concepts to liabilities.

CHAPTER OUTLINE

What factors are most important in the choice of a capital structure?

Debt capital carries more **risk**: interest is a legal obligation and could force a company into bankruptcy if these payments cannot be made

•dividends are not a legal obligation

Borrowed funds, however, can earn a higher rate of **return** to shareholders, because the company earns at a higher rate than their borrowing rate

•this is called **financial leverage**

What are liabilities, and how are they classified?

A **liability** is a probable sacrifice of economic benefits; in other words assets will be given up to satisfy it

•a liability is recorded at its current cash equivalent

•**current liabilities** will be satisfied within one year or the current operating cycle

•**noncurrent liabilities** extend beyond one year

How is liquidity measured?

The **current ratio** measures the relationship between current assets and current liabilities:

current ratio = current assets ÷ current liabilities

•may be expressed as a dollar amount (current assets - current liabilities), called **working capital**

•attempts to assess cash flow and risk characteristics

What accounts are included in current liabilities, and how are they accounted for?

Current liabilities will be satisfied within one operating cycle or one year

•**accounts payable** are debts incurred in the purchase of goods and services for resale

◊normally do not incur interest

◊often a company's largest single current liability

•**accrued liabilities** result from adjusting journal entries: **accrued expenses** incurred but not yet paid

•**income tax payable** represents taxes as yet unpaid on income earned for the year

•a number of liabilities are recorded in connection with **payroll**

◊**accrued salaries** have been earned, but not yet paid

◊various employee **benefits** are accrued: health insurance, retirement, vacations, social security tax

◊employee income taxes, deducted by the company from employees' pay

•**deferred** or **unearned revenues** are recorded when payment comes before revenues are earned

◊warranties fall under this classification, as a **future service obligation**

·estimated and accrued in the period in which the product is sold

•notes payable result from a borrowing of cash: lender willing to lend cash because they will earn interest for the use of their money

◊interest = principal * rate * time

◊interest is an expense of the period in which the money is used, recorded when incurred

•any long term debt within a year of maturity must be reclassified as current debt; known as the **current portion of long term debt**

What are long-term liabilities, and how are they accounted for?

Long term liabilities are often used to finance operational assets

•desirable to balance expected life of asset with term of loan

◊known as **secured debt** when a specific asset is pledged as security for the liability

◊**unsecured debt** has no specific asset as back-up

•a **private placement** is a borrowing directly from a financial organization

◊**note payable**, payable on a specified maturity date

•when the amount needed exceeds the capacity of a single creditor, company issues public debt known as **bonds**

What are deferred taxes?

A company's income for reporting purposes is often different from income for tax purposes, because Internal Revenue Code differs from GAAP

•income tax expense on the income statement is based on the reported income earned

•taxes payable may differ from this, because it is based on IRS rules

•reconciling account is **Deferred Taxes**, which may be an asset or a liability, but is frequently the latter

◊these are temporary, or timing, differences

How are retirement benefits accounted for?

In a **defined contribution plan**, the employer agrees to make specified cash payments to a fund, which will be available to employee upon retirement

•amount available to employee will depend on success of investment strategy of fund; employer's only obligation is to make the specified contributions

•amount contributed by employer each year is pension expense

In a **defined benefit program**, employer agrees to pay employee a specified *amount* upon retirement, based on a percentage of the person's pay at retirement, or amounts for each year of employment

•pension expense is the change in cash value of the employee's retirement package, based on

◊how close the employee is to retirement (and collection of benefits)

◊higher pay or longer service

◊life expectancy changes

•pension liability is unfunded cash value of benefits

Many employers also agree to pay **health care costs** for retirees

•cost of future benefits must be estimated and recorded as expense in period in which employees perform services for employer (and earn the benefits)

What is a contingent liability?

A **contingent liability** creates a *potential* , rather than probable, future sacrifice of economic benefits

•contingent liabilities arise because of past events

•whether a liability is recorded or contingent depends on probability of occurrence (probable, reasonably possible, or remote) and ability of management to estimate amount

◊an item probable and subject to estimate is recorded as a liability

◊items probable but not subject to an estimate are disclosed in a note

◊items reasonably possible, subject to estimate or not, are disclosed in a note

◊items only remotely possible are not required to be disclosed

How do the concepts of present and future value relate to liabilities and interest?

Present value and future value are based on the notion that money increases in value over time

> •when you know the amount of a *future* cash flow and need to determine its value *now*, you are facing a **present value** problem
>
> •when you know the value of a cash flow that occurs *today*, but must determine its value in the *future*, you have a **future value** problem
>
> •sometimes the cash flow is a **single payment**; other times a series of payments occurs, in equal amounts, evenly spaced, known as an **annuity**
>
>> ◊equal dollar amount each period
>>
>> ◊periods of equal length
>>
>> ◊consistent interest rate

In a problem asking for the **future value of a single amount**, an amount (**principal**) is invested in the present, to earn a specified **rate**, and you are to determine its value after a specified amount of **time**

> •the *present* amount is known; the *future* amount must be calculated
>
> •assumes compound interest, that is, accrued but unpaid interest earns interest
>
> •basic concept is still that interest = principal * rate * time; however for multiple periods and compound interest, repeated arithmetic computations are saved by consulting a table for the factor for the correct number of periods and the rate, and multiplying the factor found by the amount of the principal

The **present value of a single amount** is what it is worth today to have the right to receive a certain sum (principal) in the future, **discounted** (the opposite of compounded) at a specified rate, over a specified number of periods

> •the *future* amount is known, the *present* amount must be calculated

The **future value of an annuity** is calculated when you are planning to deposit a specific amount periodically and wish to know its future value at the end of the stream of payments

> •assumes that each payment is made on the last day of the period, so that the final payment made on the day the balance is computed would earn no interest

The **present value of an annuity** calculates the value *now* of a known series of amounts to be received for a specified number of periods in the future

Reference Point: Review Exhibit 9-3 in your text, which summarizes the present and future value concepts. If you have any difficulty with these concepts or their application, copy this exhibit onto a card, leaving room to jot down some examples as you work through the end-of-chapter problems assigned. This will assist you in the future when you review this material.

Interest is almost always quoted as an **annual rate**, but can be computed for any period, and interest is usually *compounded* more frequently than annually
> •if interest is compounded more frequently than annually, the interest rate, and the number of periods, must be adjusted in calculations to take this into account
>> ◊interest rate will be lowered
>> ◊number of periods will increase
>> ◊for example: a calculation at "8% interest for three years" would involve 3 periods, at 8% per period; but "8% interest *compounded quarterly* for three years" would involve 3*4 or *12* periods at 8÷4 or *2% per period*

SUPPLEMENT A
FEDERAL INCOME TAX CONCEPTS

Proprietorships and partnerships do not pay taxes as companies, but their owners pay tax on their share of the company's income as individuals
Corporations are separate entities from their owners, and pay taxes as such, based on taxable income per their income tax return, not income for reporting purposes
> •taxes = taxable income * specified rate
>> ◊rates are graded by income level so that smaller corporations pay less in taxes than large corporations
>> ◊corporations develop strategies to minimize the amount of tax they pay; tax minimization is a perfectly legal strategy; it is tax evasion that is illegal

QUESTIONS AND EXERCISES

Multiple Choice:

After considering all the possible answers to each question below, circle the letter of the *best* answer to each question. Remember that more than one answer may be *possible* in some circumstances, but only one is the *best* answer to the question.

You read about General Mills in this chapter in your text and applied liability concepts to their reported results. Let's look at a competitor in their industry, Kellogg Company. In their 1993 Annual Report, Kellogg reported current assets of $1,245.1 million, total assets of $4,237.1 million, current liabilities of $1,214.6 million, and total liabilities of $2523.7. Use this information to answer the next two questions.

1. Kellogg's current ratio at the end of 1993 was
    a. .98
    b. 1.03
    c. 30.5
    d. .5
    e. .3

2. Kellogg's working capital at the end of 1993 was
    a. $30.5
    b. $1,245.1
    c. $1,713.4
    d. $1,278.6
    e. $2,459.7

3. Deferred revenues represent a liability because
    a. no cash has been received.
    b. collection is uncertain.
    c. goods or services have been paid for, but not yet provided to the customer.
    d. the company is transferring them to another period for tax reasons.
    e. the customer may yet return the items purchased for a refund.

4. A company purchases an asset, paying a $1,000 down payment and signing a three-month note for the balance, $5,000, carrying simple interest at a nine percent annual rate. Both principal and interest will be paid in cash on the due date. Interest expense at the end of one month would be

    a. $0

    b. $37.50

    c. $112.50

    d. $450

    e. $45

5. Use the information in problem (4). At the end of the 3 months, the company will pay the lender a total of

    a. $6,112.50

    b. $5,112.50

    c. $5,450

    d. $5,135

    e. $6,135

6. Deferred taxes represent

    a. amounts resulting from the different rules used for reporting to shareholders and reporting taxes.

    b. amounts the company will pay at year-end, as opposed to during the year.

    c. amounts that the company does not have sufficient cash to pay, and must owe to the taxing authorities.

    d. reported income permanently not taxable for various reasons.

    e. taxes accrued at the end of the period with an adjusting entry, to be paid at the beginning of the following accounting period.

7. Reported pension expense for an employee under a defined benefit program resulting from a change in the cash value of the retirement package, is caused by

    a. the employee's being closer to retirement.

    b. the employee receiving higher pay or having longer service.

    c. a change in the employee's life expectancy.

    d. all of the above—a, b, and c.

    e. only a and b.

8. In order to be recorded as a liability on the balance sheet, an item must be

    a. reasonably possible and subject to estimate.

    b. probable.

    c. remote, but subject to estimate.

    d. probable, and subject to estimate.

    e. all of the above.

9. A contingent liability is one that

    a. is dependent on another company in order to occur.

    b. will result from a future event.

    c. is based on a past event and cannot be estimated.

    d. is only remotely possible, and is based on past events.

    e. creates a potential sacrifice of benefits and is based on past events.

10. A contingent liability

    a. may be recorded as a balance sheet item or as a footnote, at the discretion of the company.

    b. may be disclosed or not disclosed, at the discretion of the company.

    c. need not be disclosed at all.

    d. must be recorded as a liability if it is subject to estimate.

    e. requires disclosure in a footnote to the published statements.

11. Kellogg Company in a footnote to their 1993 Annual Report showed pension expense of $36.2 million, projected benefit obligation (pension obligation) of $337.9 million, and pension plan assets of $279.5 million for certain of their pension plans. Their liability (before a number of adjustments which they detail in the footnote) was

    a. $36.2 million.

    b. $94.6 million.

    c. $58.4 million.

    d. $337.9 million.

    e. $279.5 million.

12. An annuity is

    a. a series of annual payments of the same amount.

    b. any group of payments, equally spaced.

    c. any payments to a beneficiary from a fund set aside for that purpose.

    d. a series of consecutive equal payments, equally spaced, with the same implicit interest rate each period.

    e. annual payments of equal amounts at a fixed interest rate.

13. The present value of a known future amount

    a. will always be more than the future amount.

    b. will be equal to the future amount.

    c. will always be less than the future amount.

    d. may be greater than or less than the future amount, depending on the interest rate used.

    e. may be greater than or less than the future amount, depending on the amount of time between.

14. An example of a future value problem for a single amount is

    a. a defined benefit pension plan.

    b. a savings account to be established to fund $100,000 college tuition in 6 years.

    c. a mortgage.

    d. a Individual Retirement Account.

    e. an inheritance to be invested in a mutual fund.

Bill wants to borrow some money from Al, and has agreed to pay Al $1,000 back by the end of two years from today. Al would like to earn an 8% return on his money, compounded annually. They are trying to decide how much Bill can borrow.

15. If Bill pays Al the $1,000 in one lump sum at the end of the two years, the amount Al will be willing to lend Bill is

    a. $1,166.40

    b. $857.30

    c. $1,000

    d. $1,783.30

    e. $2,166.40

16. Refer to the information given before question 15. If Bill pays Al in two payments, one at the end of each year, of $500, Al is able to lend Bill

    a. $891.65

    b. $857.30

    c. $1,000

    d. $1,040

    e. $583.20

17. Refer again to the information before question 15. If interest were compounded semiannually instead of annually, and Bill paid Al the $1,000 in one lump sum at the end of the two years, Al would be willing to lend him

    a. $735.00

    b. $924.60

    c. $857.30

    d. $854.80

    e. $1081.60

Use this information for the next three questions:

A farmer buys a new piece of farm machinery from the local equipment outlet. He gives the dealer a down payment of $10,000, and agrees to pay them $20,000 a year from today, and another $20,000 in two years from today. The prevailing interest rate for similar transactions is 10%, compounded annually.

18. Assume that all the costs of putting this equipment into service are included in the contract shown above. The equipment should be recorded on the farmer's books of account at a cost of

    a. $34,710

    b. $50,000

    c. $44,710

    d. $40,000

    e. $41,320

199

19. Refer to the information preceding question (18). Interest expense recorded at the end of Year 1 would be

      a. $5,000

      b. $4,000

      c. $4,471

      d. $2,000

      e. $3,471

20. The net liability remaining after the first year's payment and interest are recorded is

      a. $18,181

      b. $20,000

      c. $24,710

      d. $34,710

      e. $22,000

True or False?

For each of the following statements, place the letter "T" or "F" in the space before the statement to indicate whether you think the statement is true or false. Why are the false statements *not* true? Rewrite them to make them true.

_____ 21. A liability is a probable future sacrifice of economic benefits, arising from a past transaction.

_____ 22. Current liabilities are likely to be satisfied with current assets.

_____ 23. Trade accounts payable are generally incurred as a result of the purchase of goods and services in the normal course of business.

_____ 24. An example of a deferred revenue for a retailer is the sale of furniture on a 90-day financing agreement.

_____ 25. When long-term debt, or a portion thereof, becomes due within the next year, it must be footnoted on the financial statements.

_____ 26. Companies generally use long-term debt to finance long-lived assets, matching the life of the asset to the term of the debt.

_____ 27. In a defined contribution pension plan, the employer agrees to pay the employee a fixed amount upon the employee's retirement.

_____ 28. A contingent liability with only a remote possibility of occurring must still be disclosed in a footnote if its amount can be reasonably estimated.

_____ 29. In a present value problem, you are trying to calculate the future value of a known cash flow today.

_____ 30. Since compound interest problems involve more complex interest calculations, the simple interest formula—Interest = Principal * Rate * Time—no longer holds true.

_____ 31. An individual retirement plan with a fixed annual contribution is an example of an annuity.

_____ 32. Corporate income is taxed at increasing rates depending on income level in order to decrease the burden on smaller corporations.

A Few Words from You ...

For each of the following, briefly discuss the questions, including calculations where indicated to support your answers.

33. **What does it really cost?** Your text says the following in the discussion of deferred revenues, concerning frequent flyer plans:

> Note that the amount of the liability is the incremental cost of providing free travel and not the actual selling price of an air line ticket. Some analysts believe that the true cost of frequent flyer program is the lost revenue associated with giving a ticket to a customer instead of selling it. These analysts believe that the liabilities reported for frequent flyer programs are severely understated. Currently GAAP permits recording these liabilities based on incremental cost because there is no accurate method to estimate the number of travelers who would have bought tickets if they had not earned a free award.

What do you think is the cost of providing this program? What do you think is the influence of the following:

- •Would the traveler have flown anyway, at full price?
- •What would the full price have been? Are prices uniform?
- •Did the airplane have empty seats?
- •What portion of frequent flyer points granted are redeemed?

Can you think of other factors that might be pertinent?

34. **How do these competitors compare?** In this chapter in your text, you learned about the current ratio as a test of liquidity and considered the current ratio of General Mills, based on their balance sheet in Exhibit 9-1. In questions (1) and (2) in this Study Guide, you calculated the same ratio for Kellogg. Reprinted below is the Balance Sheet for Kellogg Company at December 31, 1993 ($ millions):

Current assets

Cash and temporary investments	$ 98.1
Accounts receivable, less allowance of $6.0	536.8
Inventories:	
Raw materials and supplies	148.5
Finished goods and materials in process	254.6
Deferred income taxes	85.5
Prepaid expenses	121.6
Total current assets	1,245.1

Property	
Land	40.6
Buildings	1,065.7
Machinery and equipment	2,857.6
Construction in progress	308.6
Accumulated depreciation	(1,504.1)
Property, net	2,768.4

Intangible assets	59.1
Other assets	164.5
Total assets	$ 4,237.1

Current liabilities

Current maturities of long-term debt	$ 1.5
Notes payable	386.7
Accounts payable	308.8
Accrued liabilities:	
Income taxes	65.9
Salaries and wages	76.5
Advertising and promotion	233.8
Other	141.4
Total current liabilities	1,214.6

Long-term debt	521.6
Nonpension postretirement benefits	450.9
Deferred income taxes	188.9
Other liabilities	147.7

Shareholders' equity

Common stock, $.25 par value

Authorized: 330,000,000 shares

Issued: 310,292,753 shares	**77.6**
Capital in excess of par value	**72.0**
Retained earnings	**3,409.4**
Treasury stock, at cost: 82,372,409 shares	**(1,653.1)**
Minimum pension liability adjustment	**(25.3)**
Currency translation adjustment	**(167.2)**
Total shareholders' equity	**1,713.4**
Total liabilities and shareholders' equity	**$ 4,237.1**

Consider the current ratios and working capital positions of the two companies. How do they compare? Does it help to have actual balance sheets, and not just the ratios? Why?

A more exacting test of liquidity is a ratio known as the quick ratio, which compares quick assets—cash and equivalents and accounts receivable—to current liabilities. Calculate this ratio for each of the two companies. How do they compare?

Would you say the companies are roughly the same? Explain.

35. **What is the company liable for?** Whirlpool Corporation, in their 1993 Annual Report, says in note 13, "Contingencies,"

> The company is a party to certain financial instruments with off-balance-sheet risk primarily to meet the financing needs of its financial services customers. These financial instruments are entered into in the normal course of business and consist of lending commitments, standby letters of credit and financial guarantees.

and

> At December 31, 1993, outstanding lending commitments were $41 million and standby letters of credit, repurchase agreements and financial guarantees totaled $170 million.

Clearly the amount can be estimated. Why are these contingent liabilities, or "off-balance-sheet" items, rather than actual recorded liabilities? (You may have to look up some of their terminology in a business dictionary.)

36. **How do rate and time relate to present and future value?** Circle the correct choice to complete the following general relationships for present and future value:

a. The higher the interest rate, the (higher / lower) the present value of a known future amount.

b. The more often interest is compounded, the (higher / lower) the present value of a known future amount will be.

c. The more often interest is compounded, the (higher / lower) the future value of a known present cash flow will be.

d. The present value of an annuity of a given amount will always be (greater / less) than that amount, whereas the present value of a single sum is always (greater / less) than that sum.

e. As the number of compounding periods increases, present value (increases / decreases) but future value (increases / decreases).

Which has the greater present value: receiving $50,000 after two years, or receiving $25,000 at the end of each of the next two years? Can you explain why?

You have a choice of receiving either of the two cash flows over the next three years:

	#1	#2
Year 1	$5,000	$11,000
Year 2	$8,000	$8,000
Year 3	$11,000	$5,000

Which would you rather have? Explain.

Which has the higher present value? Explain why.

37. **Does the length of the loan make that much difference?** Your text notes in the section on long-term liabilities that long-term loans often carry different interest rates than short-term loans, simply because of their term. Check the financial pages of *The Wall Street Journal* , or call a local bank, and find out what the rates are on loans of a variety of terms. How much different are the rates? Explain why there might be differences.

38. **Categorize Kellogg's pensions.** Kellogg Company, in their 1993 Annual Report, says the following at the beginning of Note 8, "Pensions:"

> The Company has a number of U. S. and worldwide pension plans to provide retirement benefits for its employees. Benefits for salaried employees are generally based on salary and years of service, while union employee benefits are generally a negotiated amount for each year of service. Plan funding strategies are influenced by tax regulations. Plan assets consist primarily of equity securities with smaller holdings of bonds, real estate, and other investments.

Are these defined benefit plans, or defined contribution plans? Explain. What are they agreeing to give employees on retirement?

Team up!

Get together in teams of 3 - 5 members to work on each of the following:

39. **What will you have to retire on?** Reading about pensions and pension liabilities is one thing. Figuring out all the details is another. Just what is involved when an employer calculates the pension liability for an employee?

In less time than you think you will graduate from college and begin your first job, and your employer is likely to offer some form of pension plan. Suppose your employer has a pension plan that proposes to pay each vested employee, after retirement, a yearly amount equal to 60% of their average annual salary for the last five years prior to retirement. What does the employer have to consider to arrive at an amount to accrue for that employee each year? Use one member of your group as a test subject. Consider the following questions, and add any of your own that you think are pertinent. Use the present value concepts you learned in this chapter. Try to calculate an annual amount of pension expense. Then, compare your results with other groups to pool information and results. For simplicity, we will make the (probably unrealistic) assumption that you will work for the same employer your entire working life.

How much do you expect to be paid when you start working?

How long will you work?

At what age do you expect to retire (or will your employer expect you to work to before you may collect retirement benefits)?

Realistically, what will your salary increase to by the time you are ready to retire?

For how many years do you believe you will probably collect retirement pay?

How much money does that retirement pay amount to, in total?

What will be your employer's expected return on the investment of retirement funds?

Do your employer's calculations change if it is necessary to consider the fact that employees do not spend their entire working lives at one employer? What factors have to be considered because this is true?

40. **Shouldn't these be the same?** Assume you borrow $25,000, at 8% interest, compounded semiannually. The loan is to be paid back at the end of three years. Two options are available. In the first option, you will pay nothing for three years, and then pay back the entire principal and accrued interest on the last day of the third year. In the other option, you will pay $1,000 every six months for three years (6 payments), and then pay any remaining accrued liability on the last day of the three years. Have half of your team work on each option. For each option, fill out the table given below.

OPTION 1:

at the end of	beginning liability	interest expense	payment, if any	ending liability
borrowing date	---	---	---	25,000
6 months				
1 year				
1-1/2 years				
2 years				
2-1/2 years				
3 years				

OPTION 2:

at the end of	beginning liability	interest expense	payment, if any	ending liability
borrowing date	---	---	---	25,000
6 months				
1 year				
1-1/2 years				
2 years				
2-1/2 years				
3 years				

Answer the following questions based on both of your tables:

Why does the ending liability column differ in the two tables?

What is the actual meaning of the ending net liability on a particular date?

Explain compound interest. How does it affect each table?

What is the total amount of interest expense paid over the life of the loan in each option? Explain why these amounts are different.

Explain what the liability at the end of the three years consists of in each case.

And just for the fun of it ...

You keep hearing the term "derivatives" in connection with interest in the financial news. Are they some kind of esoteric bond? Have you done any reading to find out what a derivative is? Many financial writers will tell you they are not all bad.

SOLUTIONS

Multiple choice:

1. (b) 2. (a) 3. (c) 4. (b) 5. (b) 6. (a) 7. (d) 8. (d) 9. (e) 10. (e) 11. (c) 12. (d) 13. (c) 14. (e) 15. (b) 16. (a) 17. (d) 18. (c) 19. (e) 20. (a)

True or false:

21. True.

22. True.

23. True.

24. False. This revenue is not deferred, since the goods have presumably been delivered, and payment reasonably assured.

25. False. Long-term debt due within the next year must be reclassified on the balance sheet as a current liability.

26. True.

27. False. An employer with a defined contribution plan agrees to pay a specific amount into the plan in the employee's name. What the employee ultimately collects will depend further on the success of the investment of the plan assets.

28. False. A contingent liability with a remote possibility of occurring need not be disclosed.

29. False. A present value problem requires the calculation of the value today of a known future cash flow.

30. False. The formula holds for all interest calculations, simple or compound. The rate and the time are adjusted in compound interest calculations for compounding more frequently than annually.

31. True.

32. True.

A few words from you ...

36.   a. lower
        b. lower
        c. higher
        d. greater / less
        e. decreases / increases

Team up:

OPTION 1:

at the end of	beginning liability	interest expense	payment, if any	ending liability
borrowing date	---	---	---	25,000
6 months	25,000	1,000	---	26,000
1 year	26,000	1,040	---	27,040
1-1/2 years	27,040	1081.60	---	28,121.60
2 years	28,121.60	1,124.86	---	29,246.46
2-1/2 years	29,246.46	1,169.86	---	30,416.32
3 years	30,416.32	1,216.65	---	31,632.98

OPTION 2:

at the end of	beginning liability	interest expense	payment, if any	ending liability
borrowing date	---	---	---	25,000
6 months	25,000	1,000	1,000	25,000
1 year	25,000	1,000	1,000	25,000
1-1/2 years	25,000	1,000	1,000	25,000
2 years	25,000	1,000	1,000	25,000
2-1/2 years	25,000	1,000	1,000	25,000
3 years	25,000	1,000	1,000	25,000

● And just for the fun of it ...

Derivatives are a complex investing tool. That complexity is probably at the heart of their risk factor: they are not for the inexperienced. Essentially, they are a proxy for a financial instrument. The investor purchases either an obligation (future) to buy or sell a security at a certain price on a certain date, or a right (option) to purchase or sell a security over a certain period. Obviously the futures are riskier, because of the obligation to buy or sell, regardless of the success of the investor's prediction of which way the market will go. With options, all the investor stands to lose, if things don't go in the right direction, is the option premium (fee). Derivatives can be tied to anything—stocks, interest rates, other financial instruments—because they are based not on past events, but on expectations for the future. There are quite a few very informative articles in popular business publications for those who want to know more. You'll also find articles about what happens when the investment strategies of derivatives traders go very wrong, to hold down your urge to take a plunge.

CHAPTER 10

MEASURING AND REPORTING BONDS

A perfect statue never comes from a bad mold.

Chinese proverb.

OVERVIEW

In the previous chapter, we discussed many types of liabilities that are commonly found on most balance sheets. For many companies, the largest liability classification is bonds payable. In this chapter, we will examine the business purpose and accounting treatment of bonds in considerable depth. You will use the present value concepts that were introduced in the previous chapter to determine the current value of bonds. We will also discuss bond investments.

LEARNING OBJECTIVES

1. Explain the use of bonds payable by corporations.

2. Classify bonds payable.

3. Record bonds payable and interest expense.

4. Account for bonds sold at a discount.

5. Account for bonds sold at a premium.

6. Use the effective-interest method of amortization.

7. Record the early retirement of bonds.

8. Explain the use of bond sinking funds.

9. Account for bond investments held-to-maturity.

CHAPTER OUTLINE

What constitutes a company's capital structure?

Capital structure is the mixture of debt and equity used to finance a company's

operations

•**bonds** are debt securities issued to borrow large amounts of capital from more than one individual

◊traded in established exchanges once issued, so lenders can receive cash at any time

◊*liquidity* an advantage to investors who might foresee a need for their cash

◊advantage to borrowers (issuers of bonds) because it reduces the interest, or the cost of borrowing, if investors have the ability to convert the debt to cash at will

·ownership of corporation not diluted

·cash payments limited to principal and interest on loan

·interest expense tax deductible, whereas dividends are not

·**financial leverage:** the company can invest borrowed funds at a higher rate than the rate at which they borrowed

◊disadvantages of bonds are that periodic interest payments must be made, and principal must be repaid at maturity, whereas dividends are only paid when earnings are satisfactory

How do analysts judge capital structure?

Debt to equity ratio computes the ratio of funds contributed by lenders to funds contributed by owners

•company with a large ratio is called *highly leveraged*

What are the characteristics of bonds?

A **secured bond** has a specific asset as security if the borrowing company is unable to repay its debt

A **debenture** is an unsecured bond

The **bond principal** is the amount *payable at maturity*, and on which *periodic cash interest* payments are computed

•also known as **par value**, or **face value**, or **face amount**

•for most bonds it is equal to $1,000

The **stated rate** of interest is the rate at which periodic cash payments are computed

•interest usually paid annually or semiannually

•periodic cash interest payment not affected by the selling price of the bond

The **bond indenture** is the contract under which bonds are issued by a company

•contains stated rate, maturity date, dates of interest payments, and any other privileges of bondholder, as well as any restrictions on the company designed to protect bondholders' interests

 ◊**prospectus** tells potential investors about the company and the bonds

 ◊**underwriter** sells the bonds

  ·**firm commitment underwriter** buys the bonds and then resells them

  ·**best efforts underwriter** sells the bonds with no commitment to purchase them

The **bond certificate** given to the investor shows maturity date, interest rate and dates, and other provisions

A **trustee** is appointed to represent bondholders

 •ensures that all the provisions of the bond indenture are being met

Some special features can make bonds more attractive to investors

 •**callable** bonds can be retired early at *issuer* 's option

 •**redeemable** bonds can be turned in for early retirement at *bondholder* 's option

 •**convertible** bonds may be exchanged for other securities (such as common stock) of the issuer, at bondholder's option

Bonds also vary in relationship to other debt of the company

 •**senior debt** takes preference over all other debt in the event of bankruptcy or default

 •**subordinated debt** is only paid off after other specified creditors are paid

At what price will a bond be issued?

Potential investors demand a certain interest rate on their investment; this is the **market rate**, also known as the **yield**, or **effective**, or **true** rate

 •since this is the rate of return at which investors will be willing to commit their money, and the cash payments from the bond (principal and interest) are fixed by the bond certificate, the selling price of the bond must be adjusted to give investors their desired return

 •issue price of bond is the price at which the combination of cash interest payments and payment of face value at maturity will yield desired rate of return

  ◊this price is the sum of the present values of the cash interest payments (an annuity) at the desired market rate, plus the present value of the maturity value (a single sum) at the market rate

·if this price is the same as the par value, the bond is said to be issued at **par** (market rate = stated rate)

·if this price is below the par value, the bond is issued at a **discount** (market rate > stated rate)

·if this price is above par, the bond is issued at a **premium** (market rate < stated rate)

Reference Point: Exhibit 1 in your text provides a handy reference, listing many of the characteristics of bonds you will encounter in your reading. You may want to mark the page so that you can find it easily to quickly refresh your memory on a particular term.

How are bonds accounted for?

Bonds issued at **par** are recorded with a debit to cash and a credit to bonds payable, for the face amount of the issue

•bond liabilities always recorded at the present value of the future cash flows

•periodic interest payments are equal to interest expense, and are recorded with a debit to interest expense and a credit to cash

◊if (as is usually the case) interest is not paid on the last day of the company's fiscal year, an adjusting entry is necessary to accrue interest not yet paid

Bonds issued at a **discount** are recorded with the usual debit to cash; bonds payable account is credited for par value; the difference is debited to an account called **Discount on Bonds Payable**, which is a **contra liability** account

•since the company must pay back more than it received, this discount must be **amortized**—apportioned—over the life of the bond, to each interest period

◊**straight-line amortization** simply divides the discount equally between the interest periods

·the periodic amount is added to the cash interest to obtain interest expense for the period

∞credited to discount on bonds payable, thus reducing this amount

∞bond reported on balance sheet at net book value, that is, maturity value less unamortized discount

Zero coupon bonds do not pay periodic cash interest

•will sell for a very substantial discount and investor receives no payments until maturity

•accounting is the same as for a bond at a discount, but there are no cash payments to record

•book value increases every year

Bonds sell at a **premium** when the market rate is lower than the stated rate on the bonds

•difference between issue price and maturity is credited to **Premium on Bonds Payable**, an additional liability

•the premium, like a discount, must be amortized over the life of the bonds, using either the straight-line or effective interest method

What is the effective interest method of amortizing premium or discount?

Straight-line method is simple, but conceptually inaccurate; may only be used if difference from effective interest is immaterial

Under the **effective interest** method interest expense is equal to borrowing rate (market rate when bond was issued) times net liability (maturity value ± unamortized discount or premium)

•amortization of discount or premium is the difference between interest expense and cash paid

◊this amount is interest earned by bondholders but not yet (until maturity) paid to them

·a discount on a bond is an increase in interest expense for issuer, increased interest income for investor

·a premium is a decrease in interest expense for issuer, decrease in interest income for investor

How are bonds sold between interest dates   recorded?

Bonds sold between interest dates are sold for their market value plus accrued interest since the last interest date.

•at next interest date investor receives interest payment for full period

•thus issuer only has interest expense for the amount of time the cash was actually borrowed, and investors only receive income for the period during which they actually held the bonds

•company issuing bond does not have to calculate and issue checks for partial period interest

How is the early retirement of bond debt accounted for?

Company may wish, for a number of reasons, to pay off debt (called **retirement** of debt) before the maturity date;

> •frequently the indenture includes a call premium (an additional payment, usually a percent of par) in the event of early retirement
>> ◊entry must remove bond payable and any unamortized discount or premium, record cash paid, then record the difference as gain or loss on retirement
>
> •sometimes company simply buys debt back from the market, just like any other investor
>> ◊may be a wise move if bond prices have fallen
>>> ·occurs when interest rates have gone up, since bond prices move inversely to interest rates

What is a bond sinking fund?

Many indentures require company to establish a cash fund, called a **bond sinking fund**, toward repayment of the principal of a bond when due

> •assures ability to pay off debt, but managers prefer not to have it because it is an unproductive asset
>
> •often deposited with an independent trustee, who usually holds it in an interest-bearing investment
>
> •reported as a noncurrent asset

How do bonds look from the investor's side?

Investment in bonds permits manager to budget future cash flows

> •if management has the intent and the ability to hold bonds to maturity, they are called **held-to-maturity securities**
>> ◊listed at cost, adjusted for discount or premium amortization, because any unrealized gains or losses from market fluctuation will disappear at maturity when bonds are redeemed for face value
>>> ·investment account includes all incidental costs of acquiring the bonds
>>
>> ◊if bonds were acquired at par, investment account will not change over life of bonds
>>> ·interest is recorded as interest revenue

219

◊if bonds are acquired at a discount, investment account is originally debited for cost

    ·amortization of discount is credited as additional interest revenue each time interest payment is received

        ∞debited to investment account

        ∞most companies use straight-line amortization on investments

◊for bonds purchased at a premium, accounting is similar, but the investment account and interest revenue are reduced, not increased

QUESTIONS AND EXERCISES

Multiple Choice:

After considering all of the possible answers to each question below, choose the one that best answers the question. Remember that more than one answer could be possible under some circumstances, but only one answer is the best overall answer.

1. The capital structure of a company is
   a. its property, plant and equipment.
   b. the mixture of debt and equity used to finance its operations.
   c. the composition of its stockholders' equity.
   d. the different types of debt the company has outstanding.
   e. its management plan.

2. A significant advantage for the holders of bonds, as opposed to other debt, is
   a. their freedom from risk.
   b. their liquidity.
   c. their low cost.
   d. their high interest rate.
   e. their convertibility.

3. The following information is summarized from the 1993 Annual Report for The Walt Disney Company (in $millions):

Total assets	$11,751.1
Total liabilities	6,720.6
Total owners' equity	5,030.5

   Disney's debt to equity ratio for that year was
   a. .6 : 1
   b. .7 : 1
   c. 1.3 : 1
   d. .4 : 1
   e. 7 : 5

Use the following information to answer questions 4 through 13.

Scuppers Boat Works Inc. issued 200 bonds to finance expansion into a new line of designs. The bonds had a total principal of $200,000. They would pay interest semiannually at a rate of 9% per annum and will be paid off in five years. On the day the bonds were issued, January 15, 1995, similar securities were yielding a rate of 10% per annum. Scuppers' underwriter, Reedham and Ouip, purchased the entire issue to resell them to individual investors. Scuppers retained the right to buy back the bonds from the bondholders in two years at a price of $102. The bondholders may at any time trade in their bonds for common stock of Scuppers, Inc. at a rate of 50 shares of stock for each bond.

4. The par value of the bond issue is
    a. $200,000
    b. $18,000
    c. $20,000
    d. $102,000
    e. $192,275

5. The stated rate of interest on the bonds is _____%; bondholders will be paid $ _____ every _____.
    a. 9%; 18,000; year
    b. 9%; 18,000; six months
    c. 9%; 9,000; six months
    d. 10%; 10,000; six months
    e. 10%; 20,000; year

6. When Scuppers decided to issue the bonds, they would have executed a bond contract, or _____, which spelled out the terms of the bond, and any privileges and covenants.
    a. certificate
    b. debenture
    c. indenture
    d. trustee
    e. commitment

7. Since Reedham and Ouip has agreed to buy the bonds from Scuppers, they would be called a(n)

    a. indenture.

    b. trustee.

    c. investment banker.

    d. firm commitment underwriter.

    e. best efforts underwriter.

8. The provision that allows Scuppers to retire the bonds before maturity makes these ____ bonds.

    a. debenture

    b. subordinated

    c. convertible

    d. redeemable

    e. callable

9. Should Scuppers decide to redeem the bonds after two years have gone by, each individual bond will be bought back for

    a. $1,020

    b. $102

    c. $1,000

    d. $1,002

    e. $981

10. On January 15, 1995, Scuppers received _____ for these bonds.

    a. $200,000

    b. $200,207

    c. $192,414

    d. $200,212

    e. $192,275

11. The privilege of trading the bonds for common stock is called a _____ feature.
   - a. capitalizeable
   - b. retirement
   - c. callable
   - d. redeemable
   - e. convertible

12. On July 15, 1995, the bondholders will receive total cash of _____, and Scuppers will have interest expense of _____ if straight-line amortization is used.
   - a. $9,000; $9,772
   - b. $18,000; $19,545
   - c. $10,000; $9,772
   - d. $20,000; $19,545
   - e. $10,000; $9,979

13. The 10% rate for similar securities on the date of issue is known as the
   - a. stated rate.
   - b. par rate.
   - c. market rate.
   - d. coupon rate.
   - e. contract rate.

14. When a bond is issued at a discount, we know that
   - a. the company did not receive as much money as it needed.
   - b. the market rate was lower than the coupon rate.
   - c. the market rate was higher than the stated rate.
   - d. the company was not able to sell the bonds as easily as they'd anticipated.
   - e. fewer bonds were sold than were offered.

15. Cranmer Ltd. issued $1,000,000 face value bonds on June 30, 1995, for $989,469. The preferred entry to record this bond issue is

  a. Cash   1,000,000
    Bonds payable   1,000,000

  b. Cash   989,469
   Discount on bonds payable 10,531
    Bonds payable   1,000,000

  c. Cash   989,469
    Bonds payable   989,469

  d. Cash   989,469
   Premium on bonds payable 10,531
    Bonds payable   1,000,000

  e. Bonds payable   1,000,000
    Cash   1,000,000

16. If the Gorets Company issued zero coupon, 10 year bonds, with a face value of $5,000,000, and an effective yield of 12%, compounded semiannually, the cash proceeds from this issue for Gorets would be

  a. $1,559,000
  b. $5,000,000
  c. $1,610,000
  d. $4,999,970
  e. $4,949,120

17. When bonds are issued at a premium, interest expense

  a. will be equal to cash interest paid each compounding period.
  b. will be less than the cash interest paid each compounding period.
  c. will be equal to the amount of premium amortized each period.
  d. will be more than cash interest paid each compounding period.
  e. will be calculated based on the face value of the bond.

18. The effective interest method of amortizing discount or premium

a. yields a consistent dollar amount of interest each period, but a different interest rate.

b. is not materially different in most cases from the straight-line method.

c. yields a consistent interest rate each period, but a different dollar amount of interest expense.

d. divides the discount or premium into equal amounts for each year of the bond's life.

e. calculates interest expense based on the net liability and the coupon interest rate.

19. Ides Company sold $300,000 of 8% stated rate 5-year bonds on March 1, 1995, when the market rate was 10%. The bonds were issued to pay interest semiannually on June 30 and December 31. Accrued interest paid by the investors at the time of purchase was

a. $24,000

b. $12,000

c. $5,000

d. $4,000

e. $4,614

20. When the Ides Company in question (19) pays interest on June 30, the debit(s) will be to

a. interest expense.

b. interest expense and premium on bonds payable.

c. interest expense and interest receivable.

d. interest expense and interest payable.

e. interest payable.

21. Blazing Lasers Co. retired $400,000 face value of bonds on June 30, 1995, when the discount on bonds payable account had a balance of $32,495. They paid $360,000 to retire the bonds. Their income statement would show, for this transaction,

a. a gain of $72,475.

b. a loss of $40,000

c. a gain of $40,000.

d. a loss of $7,505.

e. a gain of $7,505.

22. Willow Co. purchased 7% coupon rate bonds with a face value of $800,000. They paid $740,000 for these bonds. The bonds will mature in 10 years, and pay interest semiannually. The entry to record this purchase would be

    a. Held-to-maturity investment 800,000

        Cash   800,000

    b. Held-to-maturity investment 740,000

        Cash   740,000

    c. Bonds receivable   800,000

        Discount on bonds receivable   60,000

        Cash   740,000

    d. Bonds receivable   800,000

        Premium on bonds receivable   60,000

        Cash   740,000

    e. Held-to-maturity investment 800,000

        Cash   740,000

        Gain on purchase of investment   60,000

23. When they receive their first interest payment, Willow Co. in problem (22) above will make the following entry:

a. Cash   28,000

    Interest revenue   28,000

b. Cash   56,000

    Interest revenue   56,000

c. Cash   28,000

    Held-to-maturity investment 3,000

        Interest revenue   31,000

d. Cash   56,000

    Held-to-maturity investment 6,000

        Interest revenue   62,000

e. Cash   25,900

    Held-to-maturity investments3,000

        Interest revenue   28,900

True or False?

For each of the following statements, place the letter "T" or "F" in the space before the statement to indicate whether you think the statement is true or false. Think about *why* each statement you mark with an "F" is false. Reword each statement you've marked "false" to make it true, to be sure you understand the concept.

_____ 24. One disadvantage of bonds, compared to stock, for financing a company's operations is that dividends on stock are discretionary, whereas bond interest must be paid.

_____ 25. Financial leverage is the ratio of debt to equity financing.

_____ 26. A debenture is another word for any bond.

_____ 27. An independent trustee is appointed in a bond issue to control the money raised and the payment of interest and principal.

_____ 28. When a company issues bonds, it tries to set the coupon rate on the bond slightly higher than the market rate so that the bond can be issued at a premium and they will receive more money.

_____ 29. The par value of a bond is a minimum legal amount below which the bond cannot be issued.

_____ 30. A zero coupon bond is one on which no periodic cash interest payments are made.

_____ 31. Straight-line amortization of discount or premium is simpler, but the effective interest method is conceptually preferable.

_____ 32. The net liability of a bond at any point in time is the present value of the future cash flows from the bond, discounted at the market interest rate on the date of issue of the bond.

_____ 33. The sum of the cash interest payments less the premium on the bond payable on the date of issue is the total interest expense on the bond.

_____ 34. A call premium, stated as a percentage of par value, is often included in the bond indenture in the event that bonds are retired before their maturity date.

_____ 35. A bond sinking fund is always established as part of the bond indenture to provide for the retirement of the bonds at maturity.

_____ 36. For an investor, bonds are always classified as held-to-maturity securities, because they have a definite maturity date.

A Few Words from You ...

Briefly explain each of the issues posed below. Use calculations to support your answers where indicated.

37. **What are the advantages and disadvantages?** Each element of a company's capital structure—bonds and stocks—has its advantages and disadvantages. On the chart below, a number of the advantages and disadvantages are listed. In each column write "Y" or "N" to indicate whether the item is an advantage (or a disadvantage as the case may be) to stocks and to bonds.

	Stocks	Bonds
a. Liquid: traded on established exchanges.		
b. Dilutes ownership of the company.		
c. Cash payments limited to specified interest, regardless of net income growth.		
d. Payments are tax deductible.		
e. Positive financial leverage is possible.		
f. Interest payments must be made.		
g. Initial amount invested must be paid back.		
h. Investors receive a return only if earnings are satisfactory.		

38. **How do they pay for all those new restaurants?** The following condensed figures were taken from the 1992 Annual Report of McDonald's Corporation:

	1992	**1991**
Total assets	$ 11,681.2	$11,349.1
Current liabilities	1,544.6	1,287.9
Noncurrent liabilities	4,244.2	5,226.1
Stockholders' equity	5,892.4	4,835.1

Calculate McDonald's debt to equity ratio.

Comment on this ratio. Does it seem high? Low? Is this a company that you would expect to have need for long-term financing? Explain.

How do you think McDonald's finances its growth?

Do you think that the general level of the debt to equity ratio is a matter of individual corporate philosophy?

39. **What can you learn from this table?** Consider the following amortization table for a bond:

period	begin liability	interest expense	cash interest	disc/prem amortized	face value	unamort.'d disc. / prem.	ending liability
issue, 4/1/95	---	---	---	---	100,000	2619	102,619
9/30/95	102,619	4105	4500	395	100,000	2224	102,224
3/31/96	102,224	4089	4500	411	100,000	1813	101,813
9/30/96	101,813	4073	4500	427	100,000	1386	101,386
3/31/97	101,386	4055	4500	445	100,000	941	100,941
9/30/97	100,941	4038	4500	462	100,000	479	100,479
3/31/98	100,479	4019	4500	481	100,000	< 2 >*	99,998*

*Error is due to rounding. A company would perform calculations to the penny, and adjust the final period's interest expense if necessary for any rounding error. The error was left here so that calculations can be easily traced by the student.

Answer the following questions based on the information in the table:

Fill in the dollar amounts on the following time line cash flow diagram for this bond:

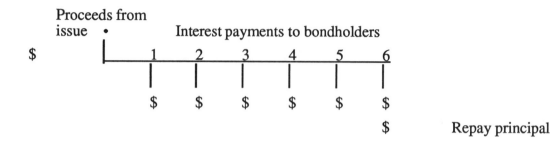

Proceeds from issue

$

Interest payments to bondholders

1   2   3   4   5   6

$ $ $ $ $ $

$ Repay principal

What is the total amount of cash received by the issuer of the bonds?

What is the total amount of cash paid to bondholders by the issuer?

What is the total amount of interest expense over the life of the bonds?

What is the coupon rate of the bonds?

What was the market rate on the date of issue of the bonds?

How often is interest compounded?

Was this bond issued at a premium or a discount? Explain why you think so.

Explain exactly what the net liability at the end of each period is. Explain it as though you are talking to a stockholder who really does not understand any of the accounting for bonds.

Why is the net liability decreasing?

Why is interest expense less than the cash interest the company is paying? Do they overpay on purpose?

● Where in the financial statements does the ending liability each period appear, and how is it presented?

What is the unamortized discount / premium? What kind of account is it? How does it affect the company's debt?

This company has a fiscal year that conforms to the calendar year. What entry would they have to make at December 31, 1995? (You should be able to calculate all the numbers you need.) Why is this entry necessary?

● How would this bond be listed in the business press?

40. **Just right for them?** A few years ago, the Tennessee Valley Authority, a large power company, issued some 50-year maturity bonds, including zero coupon bonds. Although there were some doubts at the time about the company's ability to sell bonds with such a long life, the bonds as a matter of fact sold very well indeed. Most were purchased by pension plans.

Explain why an issuing company might want such a distant maturity on its bonds. Do you think the type of company has anything to do with this? Why do you think they needed the money?

●

Explain why a 50-year bond might be considered difficult to sell.

In this and the previous chapter you have studied both bonds and pension liabilities. Why would these 50-year bonds be so attractive to pension funds?

Team up!

Get together in teams of 3 - 5 members to decide each of the following:

41. **How active are bonds?** Choose a number of companies' bonds from *The Wall Street Journal*, perhaps eight or ten companies. You may want to have a "theme" for your choices, that is, all the companies will be in the same industry, or all competitors, or all companies in your geographic area, or perhaps you want to use the companies found in examples in your text and this workbook. Follow these bonds for a week (two, if you are going to spend more time on this chapter).

For each company:

What is the coupon rate?

What is the yield, or effective rate?

How close to maturity are the bonds?

Chart the selling price of the bonds. How is it changing?

How many bonds are being sold each day?

Now compare your companies.

How do you explain the differences in coupon rates? in activity?

● Have there been any news items in the paper about any of your companies? Have these events affected the behavior of their bonds? Explain.

Have there been events in the market in general that have had a noticeable effect on all the bonds? What were the events? What was their effect?

42. **What if you bought one of these bonds?** Choose one of the corporate bonds you have been watching. Suppose you purchased it on the open market on one of the dates you recorded (just one bond—you don't have too much money to spend).
How much will you have to pay for the bond?

Show how the bond will be reported on your balance sheet.

●

Assume for simplicity that you bought the bond just after an interest date. Six months (or a year) go by, and it is time for you to receive your first interest payment. (Can you tell from the listing in the newspaper which bonds are annual, and which semiannual? It's there!) How much interest will you receive? What is your interest revenue? How will you journalize the receipt?

How will your purchase of the bond affect the company that issued the bond?

How will *your* interest revenue compare to the *interest expense* of the company that issued the bond?

●

235

And just for the fun of it ...

For a little light reading with a plot that revolves around the pitfalls of firm commitment underwriting, you might enjoy Ken Follett's "A Dangerous Fortune," published in 1993 by Delacorte Press. It has a good plot with business undertones.

SOLUTIONS

Multiple choice:

1. (b) 2. (b) 3. (c) 4. (a) 5. (c) 6. (c) 7. (d) 8. (e) 9. (a) 10. (e) 11. (e) 12. (a) 13. (c) 14. (c) 15. (b) 16. (a) 17. (b) 18. (c) 19. (d) 20. (d) 21. (e) 22. (b) 23. (c)

True or false:

24. True.

25. False. Financial leverage is the ability of a company to invest borrowed money at a rate of return higher than their borrowing rate, thus increasing return to stockholders.

26. False. A debenture is an unsecured bond. Some bonds are secured by specific assets, and thus are not debentures.

27. False. An independent trustee is appointed to monitor the interests of the bondholders.

28. False. The company chooses a coupon rate that they believe will be equal to the expected market rate on the date of issue, and does not "try" for either a discount or a premium.

29. False. The par value is the face value of the bond, and it might well be issued at that value or below.

30. True.

31. True.

32. True.

33. True.

34. True.

35. False. A bond sinking fund may or may not be required by the bond contract.

36. False. Bonds are the only security that *can* be classified as held-to-maturity, but they only have this classification if the company has the *ability* and *intent* to hold them to maturity.

A few words ...
37.

	Stocks	Bonds
a.	Y	Y
b.	Y	N
c.	N	Y
d.	N	Y
e.	N	Y
f.	N	Y
g.	N	Y
h.	Y	N

38. debt to equity ratio = (1992) $5788.8 \div 5892.4 = .98 : 1$
                            (1991) $6514 \div 4835.1 = 1.35 : 1$

CHAPTER 11

MEASURING AND REPORTING OWNERS' EQUITY

Did you ever expect a corporation to have a conscience, when it has no soul to be damned, and no body to be kicked?
Edward, First Baron Thurlow
(written in the last quarter of the 18th century)

OVERVIEW

In the previous two chapters, we discussed accounting and business issues related to funds provided by creditors. In this chapter, we will examine issues pertaining to funds provided by the owners of a business. We will focus primarily on the corporate form, the most prominent type of business in this country.

LEARNING OBJECTIVES

1. Describe the basic nature of a corporation.

2. Compare and contrast the various types of capital stock.

3. Record transactions affecting capital stock.

4. Define and account for treasury stock.

5. Account for dividends on common and preferred stock.

6. Contrast and account for stock dividends and stock splits.

7. Measure and report retained earnings.

8. Discuss the differences between corporations, proprietorships, and partnerships.

CHAPTER OUTLINE

What are the characteristics of a corporation?

Not all businesses are corporations, but they are the dominant form of business in terms of volume, because of the ease of ownership

•people can be part owners by buying shares in small amounts

•ownership easily transferred, by selling shares in established markets

•stockholders' liability to creditors is limited to the assets of the corporation

Corporation is a separate legal entity

•continuous existence, separate from owners

•incurs debts, owns assets, enters into contracts

Owner of a corporation is known as a **stockholder** or **shareholder**, with certain rights

•vote at stockholders' meeting or by **proxy** (in essence, an absentee ballot)

•participate in profits

•share assets on liquidation

•maintain percentage of ownership by purchasing shares in any new issue in proportion to current number of shares owned

Corporation is created by applying to the appropriate state official

•corporations are regulated by state (not federal) governments

•state issues a **charter**, or articles of incorporation

◊corporation is governed by a board of directors elected by stockholders

·generally, the board appoints a president who in turn employs senior managers below him

◊charter specifies **authorized shares** of stock, that is, maximum number of shares that can be issued

·if the company wants to issue more than this it must amend the charter, with stockholders' permission

◊shares never yet sold to the public are called **unissued shares**

◊**issued shares** have been sold

◊**outstanding shares** are issued shares that the company has not bought back

How many types of capital stock are there?

Most references to "stock" mean **common stock**

•must be issued by all corporations, and before any other type of stock is issued

•dividend rate determined by board of directors, based on profitability

•most states require common stock to have a **par value**, which sets a permanent amount of capital—**legal capital**—that owners cannot withdraw

◊nominal value established by the charter

•states that allow **no-par-value** stock usually have legal capital defined by law

•legal capital cannot be used for dividends

Preferred stock has some of the features of bonds, and some of the features of stock

- usually does not have voting rights
- may be no-par, but typically has a par value
- most often has a fixed dividend rate
- less risky than common because it receives priority on dividends, that is, preferred dividends have to be paid before any common dividends can be paid
- usually has a specified amount per share to be received in a liquidation
- often also carries special features
    - ◊**convertible** preferred can be exchanged for shares in the company
    - ◊**callable** preferred can be bought back by the corporation at their option, at a call price, usually above par

How is capital stock accounted for?

Stockholders' equity has two sources of capital

- paid in, or **contributed**, capital comes from the sale of stock to investors
    - ◊amounts equal to par value times shares sold
    - ◊paid-in capital in excess of par value
- retained earnings is the cumulative amount generated from the company's profit-making activities
    - ◊primary source of most companies' equity

An **initial public offering (IPO)** is the first sale of the company's stock to the public; a **seasoned new offering** is a subsequent sale of new stock

- most sales of stock are for cash
    - ◊credits to common stock, and capital in excess of par
- sales between investors are not recorded by the company
    - ◊done on **secondary markets**, such as New York Stock Exchange **(NYSE)**, American Stock Exchange **(AMEX)**, and over-the-counter **(OTC)** markets
    - ◊not recorded by the company but of interest to managers as an indicator of public perception of the success of the company
- when stock is issued to acquire an asset, or services, it should be recorded at the market value of the stock on the date of issue
    - ◊if market value of stock cannot be determined, the market value of the goods or services is used

240

What is treasury stock?

Stock issued to stockholders, then re-acquired by the company is called **treasury stock**

- company may want to have stock on hand for a bonus plan
- while it is in the treasury, the stock has no stockholder rights
- stock carried at its cost in an account called **Treasury Stock**
    - ◊this account is *not an asset* ; it is a stockholder's equity contra account
        - ·since the stock is no longer outstanding, it is subtracted from equity
    - ◊if the stock is subsequently resold, no gain or loss is reported
        - ·if a gain is realized—that is, the stock is resold for more than its cost—an account named "contributed capital from treasury stock transactions" is credited
        - ·if a loss occurs, this account is debited to the extent of its balance; if the balance is insufficient, then retained earnings is debited

How are dividends accounted for?

Return on common stock can come from appreciation in value and from **dividends**

- companies differ in dividend policy, from growing companies who reinvest earnings and pay no dividends, to utilities who often pay especially high dividends
- corporation has no legal obligation to declare dividends
- dividend must be approved by board of directors
    - ◊liability created as soon as the board declares the dividend
    - ◊recorded as a debit to retained earnings and credit to dividend payable
- "dividend" usually means a **cash dividend** unless otherwise specified
    - ◊company can also issue a **stock dividend**, that is, a payment in its own stock
- two fundamental requirements for a cash dividend
    - ◊sufficient retained earnings
    - ◊sufficient cash
- three significant dates for a dividend
    - ◊date of **declaration**, when board declares the dividend
    - ◊date of **record**, or date on which stockholder has to own stock to receive dividend
    - ◊date of **payment**, when cash is paid to stockholders of record

How are the dividends on preferred stock measured and paid?

Preferred stockholders give up certain advantages

•they have **no vote**

•their **dividends are fixed** by contract, so they do not increase if earnings increase

However preferred stockholders have compensating advantages

•dividend **preference**

◊**current** dividend preference: the preferred dividend has to be paid before any common dividends are paid

◊**cumulative preference**: if the preferred stock is cumulative, the company has to keep track of **dividends in arrears** for any year in which no, or only a partial, preferred dividend is declared and paid

·must pay dividends in arrears plus current preferred dividend before any common dividends are paid

·dividends in arrears are a memo account, not reported on balance sheet, since dividends are not a liability until declared

---

Reference point: Review Exhibit 4 in your text at this point. Preferred and common dividend payments under a number of scenarios are illustrated.

How do stock dividends work?

A **stock dividend** is a distribution of additional shares of the company's stock to existing shareholders

•done on a pro rata basis, that is, stockholders receive shares in proportion to what they already own as a percentage of total shares outstanding

◊has no economic value in and of itself, since stockholder still owns the same percentage of the company, but it is represented by more shares of stock

◊market immediately reacts, and the price of the stock decreases proportionately, since no wealth was added

in reality, the drop is not always precisely proportionate because the lower price may make the stock more attractive to investors, increasing demand and causing price to rise

242

•large stock dividend is more than 20 or 25% of the outstanding shares

◊journal entry transfers from retained earnings to common stock an amount equal to the par value of the shares

•small stock dividend is less than 20 or 25% of outstanding shares

◊journal entry transfers from retained earnings, to common stock and additional paid in capital, an amount equal to the market value of the shares

What is a stock split?

A **stock split** looks similar to a stock dividend, but affects the balance sheet differently

•total number of authorized shares is increased

•old shares are called in and replaced by a greater number of new shares

•par value is reduced so that *total* par value of *all* shares is unchanged

•requires no journal entry, but is disclosed in notes

•neither a stock split nor a stock dividend changes total stockholders' equity

How are retained earnings accounted for?

Retained earnings are the accumulated income of the company, less dividends, since it began

•**prior period adjustment** may occasionally be made to beginning retained earnings: correction of an accounting error that occurred in financial statements of a previous period

◊cannot be corrected in current income statement because it would distort current period's earnings

•sometimes **restrictions** are placed on retained earnings that limit the company's ability to pay dividends

◊typically happens when a company borrows money, to safeguard creditor's ability to obtain repayment

◊full disclosure principle requires that restrictions be disclosed in statements or footnotes

How does the accounting for unincorporated businesses differ from that for corporations?

Proprietorship has one owner; **partnership** has two or more owners

•most accounting is the same, except for owners' equity

◊proprietorships and partnerships have no capital stock or retained earnings

·use capital account(s) for increases to investment, or earnings

·drawing account(s) for owner's(s') withdrawals of cash or other assets

---

Reference point: For a useful summary of the account structure of all three types of business organization, see Exhibit 5 in your text. Supplement A to the chapter discusses partnership and proprietorship equity in more detail.

SUPPLEMENT A
ACCOUNTING FOR OWNERS' EQUITY FOR SOLE PROPRIETORSHIPS AND PARTNERSHIPS

How does owners' equity for a sole proprietorship look?

A **proprietorship** needs a **capital** account for the proprietor, and a **drawing** (withdrawals) account

    •**capital** account records investments and accumulates periodic income or loss
    •**drawing** account is used to record withdrawals by the owner of cash or other assets
        ◊closed to the capital account at the end of each period
Proprietorship does not pay taxes, so there is no tax liability
    •taxes for the business are reported on the owner's personal return
    •the owner's "salary" is not an expense of the business, but rather a withdrawal (owner cannot be his/her own employee)

What is the accounting for partnership owners' equity?

A **partnership** is two or more persons agreeing to pursue some business
    •agreement should be in writing
    •this form of business has certain advantages
        ◊ease of formation
        ◊control by partners (no stockholders or board of directors)
        ◊no income taxes on the business (just on partners as individuals)
    •primary disadvantage is unlimited liability of partners for the business debts
    •accounting is similar to that for proprietorships, except that each partner has individual capital and drawing accounts

QUESTIONS AND EXERCISES

Multiple Choice:

Consider all the choices following each question below. Choose the best answer for the question.

1. A stockholder of a corporation is
    a. one of the owners of the corporation.
    b. a creditor of the corporation.
    c. both an owner and a creditor of the corporation.
    d. a manager of the corporation.
    e. both c and d.

2. In order to create a corporation, it is necessary to apply to
    a. the federal government.
    b. the appropriate office in the state in which the corporation will be organized.
    c. the SEC.
    d. the FASB.
    e. the IRS.

3. Outstanding shares of stock are those which
    a. have been issued to investors.
    b. have been issued, and have not been bought back by the company.
    c. the company is permitted by its charter to issue.
    d. are authorized, but have not yet been issued.
    e. have been repurchased by the company.

On the 1994 balance sheet of J. C. Penney Company, the following information is listed in the stockholders' equity section, :

> Preferred stock, without par value:
> Authorized, 25 million shares—issued, 1 million shares
> of Series B LESOP convertible preferred

(LESOP means leveraged employee stock ownership plan.) Use this information to answer the next two questions.

4. The notation on the stock indicates that the stock can

    a. be exchanged for the company's common stock.

    b. be exchanged for the company's bonds.

    c. be redeemed at the will of the holders.

    d. be retired at the option of the company.

    e. receive dividends from prior periods in which no dividends were paid.

5. Since the stock is listed with no par value, and thus no way to calculate a dividend rate, it is likely that dividends on this stock

    a. are not paid.

    b. are the same as common stock dividends.

    c. are specified on the shares themselves, and explained in a footnote to the balance sheet.

    d. must be set by the board of directors.

    e. must be put to a vote of shareholders.

6. Caldor Corporation, in their 1994 Annual Report, listed the following in stockholders' equity:

    Common stock, par value $.01 – authorized, 50,000,000 shares; issued and outstanding, 16,697,467

Their total paid in capital at that time was $199,623 (they express all amounts rounded to thousands).

The dollar amount shown in the Common stock account would be

    a. $500

    b. $200

    c. $167

    d. $199

    e. $333

7. Refer to the information in question (6). The average price received by Caldor for a share of stock

    a. was $.01

    b. was $3.99

    c. was $21.13

    d. cannot be calculated from the information given.

    e. was $11.96

8. Assume that Caldor in question (6) sold 1,200 shares of stock at a price of $30 per share during 1994. The entry to record this transaction would be

a.
	Cash	36,000	
	Common stock		36,000

b.
	Cash	36,000	
	Common stock		12
	Income from stock sale		35,988

c.
	Cash	36,000	
	Common stock	12	
	Retained earnings	35,988	

d.
	Cash	36,000	
	Common stock	12	
	Additional paid-in capital	35,988	

e.
	Cash	12	
	Common stock		12

9. Quinn had one hundred shares of Caldor common stock that she had purchased for $21 per share. She sold the shares to Randy for $28 per share. On *Caldor's* books this would

a. be shown as an increase in stockholders' equity of $2800.

b. be shown as an increase in stockholders equity of $700.

c. be shown as an increase in retained earnings of $700.

d. be shown as an increase to additional paid-in capital of $700.

e. not be shown at all.

10. In Town, a new company publishing a guide for newcomers to a large city, offered a local print shop 25 shares of their $1 par common stock, in lieu of cash, for printing flyers introducing their new magazine to area businesses. Some of their shares had recently been bought for $10 apiece. The printer would normally have charged $275 for the printing. The transaction should be recorded as follows:

a.
Printing expense	250	
Common stock		25
Additional paid-in capital		225

b.
Printing expense	275	
Common stock		25
Additional paid-in capital		250

c.
Printing expense	275	
Common stock		25
Additional paid-in capital		225
Retained earnings		25

d.
Printing expense	250	
Common stock		250

e.
Printing expense	275	
Common stock		275

11. Refer to the information in problem 10. Assume that the recently sold shares were bought by the founder of In Town, and no established market price for the stock existed. Under these circumstances, the transaction described (stock for printing services) would be valued at

a. $250

b. $0

c. $275

d. $25

e. a negotiated price, agreed on by the buyer and the seller.

Butterscotch Cosmic Treats Co. purchased 40,000 shares of its own $1 par common stock on the open market for $600,000. They intend to hold the stock for employee bonuses. Use this information to answer the next two questions.

12. This stock would be carried on the Butterscotch books as
    a. a contra equity account.
    b. additional common stock issued.
    c. an asset, at cost.
    d. an asset, at par value.
    e. a liability.

13. The following quarter, Butterscotch had an opportunity to sell 10,000 of the shares for $18 apiece. The entry to record this sale would be

    a. Cash   150,000
            Treasury stock   150,000

    b. Cash   180,000
            Treasury stock   10,000
            Capital in excess of par   140,000
            Gain on treasury stock   30,000

    c. Cash   180,000
            Treasury stock   150,000
            Gain on sale of treasury stock 30,000

    d. Cash   180,000
            Treasury stock   150,000
            Contributed capital, treasury
                stock transactions   30,000

    e. Cash   180,000
            Treasury stock   150,000
            Retained earnings   30,000

14. On December 31, 1995, the board of directors of Ardent Inc. issued a press release to the newspapers stating that the company planned to pay a dividend of $.12 per share on its common stock. The date of this announcement is known as the date of _____ ; the company must record a liability _____ .

    a. record; on the date of declaration.

    b. record; on the date of record.

    c. declaration; in the year in which the dividend will be paid.

    d. declaration; on the date of declaration.

    e. dividend; when the books are closed for the fiscal year.

15. Ardent Inc. had 1,000 shares of $100 par, 6% preferred stock outstanding, as well as 100,000 shares of $.01 par common stock. On March 31, 1996, their year-end, they declared a dividend of $9,500. In the past, they have tried to maintain a minimum dividend of $.10 per share on common stock. For the March 31 dividend, preferred stockholders would receive a total of _____ and common stockholders a total of _____ .

    a. $6,000; $10,000

    b. $0; $9,500

    c. $4,750; $4,750

    d. $0; $10,000

    e. $6,000; $3,500

16. Refer to the information in question 15. Suppose the preferred stock is cumulative, and Ardent, having had a slow year, was unable to pay any dividends last year . In that case, preferred stock would receive _____ and common stock _____ on March 31 of this year.

    a. $6,000; $3,500

    b. $12,000; 0

    c. $9,500; 0

    d. $12,000; $10,000

    e. $4,750; $4,750

17. On January 31, 1995, Paddington Enterprises, Ltd. declared a 15% stock dividend to its shareholders. At that time Paddington had 300,000 shares of $1 par common stock outstanding, and the market price of a share on that day was $22. What is the entry to record this transaction?

    a.   Retained earnings   45,000

                  Common stock   45,000

    b.   Retained earnings   990,000

                  Dividend payable   990,000

    c.   No entry is made to record a small stock dividend.

    d.   Retained earnings   990,000

                  Common stock   45,000

                  Additional paid in capital   945,000

    e.   Retained earnings   990,000

                  Common stock   45,000

                  Cash   945,000

18. A stock split, unlike a stock dividend,
    a. requires no journal entry.
    b. does not change total stockholders' equity.
    c. reduces the par value of the stock.
    d. increases the total number of shares outstanding.
    e. both (a) and (c).

19. A prior period adjustment resulting from an error discovered after a previous year's results have been published is made
    a. to the ending balance of retained earnings.
    b. to the beginning balance of retained earnings.
    c. only in a footnote, not to the actual financial statements.
    d. to the income statement of the current period, as a extraordinary item.
    e. by doing over the financial statements of the relevant year, and re-releasing them.

20. Income earned by a sole proprietorship is contained in the
    a. retained earnings account.
    b. income summary account.
    c. owner's capital account.
    d. capital stock account.
    e. drawing account.

21. The accounting for the owners' equity of a partnership is similar to that for a proprietorship, except that
    a. each partner has his/her own individual capital and drawing accounts.
    b. the capital and drawing accounts contain shares for all the partners, with divisions maintained on a memo basis.
    c. a partnership has a retained earnings account.
    d. capital stock accounts are set up for the partners.
    e. drawing accounts are not permitted.

True or False?

For each of the following statements, place the letter "**T**" or "**F**" in the space before the statement to indicate whether you think the statement is true or false. Reword each false statement, making it true, to be sure you understand the concept.

_____ 22. The number of authorized shares in a corporation refers to the original number of shares issued when that company "went public."

_____ 23. If a corporation only has one class of stock, it is common stock.

_____ 24. Legal capital is a permanent amount of capital that owners cannot withdraw.

_____ 25. Unlimited liability refers to the fact that creditors of a liquidated corporation can put claims on the assets of shareholders for debts that corporate assets are insufficient to pay.

_____ 26. The chief advantage of preferred stock is that its dividends must be paid before any dividends can be given to common shareholders.

_____ 27. Contributed capital from the sale of stock with a par value is usually divided between amounts received equal to par value of the shares sold, and amounts received in excess of par.

_____ 28. When shareholders in a corporation sell all or part of their holdings to other private individuals, no entry is required on the part of the corporation.

_____ 29. Treasury stock consists of unissued shares of the company's stock.

_____ 30. When no other qualifying statements are made, the term "dividend" can mean either a cash or a stock dividend.

_____ 31. A large stock dividend is recorded at the par value of the shares distributed.

_____ 32. A stock split results in a decrease in the par value of the stock, and a proportionate increase in the number of shares outstanding.

_____ 33. The full disclosure principle requires that any restrictions on retained earnings be reported on the financial statements.

A Few Words from You ...

For each of the following questions, explain the issues involved briefly, using calculations to support your answer where required.

34. **Why do they still want the stock?** If a company has cumulative preferred stock outstanding, with dividends in arrears, your text notes that this could be a concern to common shareholders, impeding their ability to collect dividends on their stock. In this case, why would a shareholder still consider it an advantage to continue to hold the common stock?

35. **Is this still a dividend?** Explain, considering the source of the funds, why it is not only generally illegal, but also illogical to declare a dividend and pay that dividend out of additional paid in capital, lacking retained earnings. Isn't the company still "giving something" to its shareholders?

36. **Decoding stockholders' equity?** Below is the actual stockholders' equity section from the 1994 Annual Report of J. C. Penney Company, Inc. (dollar amounts in millions):

Stockholders' Equity

Preferred stock, without par value:	
Authorized, 25 million shares – issued, 1 million shares	
of Series B LESOP convertible preferred	$ 630
Guaranteed LESOP obligation	(307)
Common stock, par value 50¢:	
Authorized, 1,250 million shares –	
issued 227 million shares shares	1,030
Reinvested earnings	4,262
Total stockholders' equity	$ 5,615

What kind of account would you call the "Guaranteed LESOP obligation", based on the way the dollar amount is listed? (Don't worry about *what* it really is.)

What is reinvested earnings?

Where is their additional paid in capital (capital in excess of par)?

● Is this presentation of the capital stock account and additional paid in capital in conformity with what you view as full disclosure? In other words, can reasonably informed readers obtain the information they need?

Why do you think the company would have so many more authorized shares than they apparently need or intend to issue? What effect do all these extra shares have on stockholders' equity?

37. **The Gap, Inc.** Shown below is a portion of the stockholders' equity section from the 1993 Annual Report of The Gap, Inc. (dollar amounts in thousands):

● **Stockholders' Equity**

Common stock $.05 par value

Authorized 500,000,000 shares; issued 155,733,256 shares	$ 7,787
Additional paid-in capital	240,655
Retained earnings	1,026,836
Foreign currency translation adjustment	(8,314)
Restricted stock plan deferred compensation	(48,035)
Total Stockholders' Equity	$ 1,218,929

Suppose The Gap decided subsequent to this statement to declare a cash dividend of $.10 per share of common stock. Rewrite the stockholders' equity section, giving effect to this transaction.

Go back to the original statement. Suppose, instead, that The Gap declared a 100% stock dividend. Again, rewrite the stockholders' equity statement, giving effect to this transaction.

Return once again to the original statement. This time rewrite the statement as though The Gap had declared a two-for-one stock split.

Compare the three statements you have written. How do they differ? How are they the same?

What was the effect of each transaction on *total stockholders' equity* ? Explain why the effects you found are true.

● Suppose an individual shareholder owned 100 shares of The Gap. How would each of these transactions affect that person?

How would each of these transactions affect the *total market value* of The Gap stock?

How would each of these transactions affect the market value of *one share* of The Gap stock?

● Finally, again return to the original stockholders' equity section at the beginning of this problem. Suppose The Gap acquired 10,484,528 shares of treasury stock for a cost of $92,454,000. Redo the stockholders' equity section of their balance sheet, giving effect to the treasury stock.

Team up!

By now you may have a group of people you work with regularly on team assignments.

● Decide the following questions together.

38. **How much do you really own?** Choose a number of companies, perhaps 15 - 20 so that you can have a broad cross section. Select companies that vary in size. Each of you can research four or five companies. Suppose your group owns 100 shares of each company. Just what does this amount to? Consider the following questions.
What percentage of the company does your "hundred block" represent?

How much influence will your 100 shares have in terms of voting in the shareholders' meeting?

What do your 100 shares represent in terms of total earnings for the most current year?

What are the dividends on your 100 shares?

What is the market value of your 100 shares?

What is the par value of your 100 shares?

What is the book value—net stockholders' equity per share—of your 100 shares?

39. **Is it dividends you want?** Choose a group of companies again. You could probably use some of the same companies you chose if you did question (38). This time, you want a number of different *types* of companies represented: retailers, manufacturers, service, high-tech, utilities, transportation, entertainment, communications. There are more choices than you will want to gather, so just look at 4 or 5 companies from perhaps 4 or 5 groups. For each company, examine the amount of dividend the company pays. You may want to "even the field" by calculating dividend payout ratio, that is, dividend per share ÷ earnings per share, and dividend yield, that is, dividend per share ÷ price per share.
How do the companies compare?

Is there any pattern identifiable by industry?

Is there any relationship between the amount of dividends paid and the growth in the same period in the value of the stock?

40. **What kind of business will you be?** Suppose one member of your group begins a proprietorship by investing $5,000 of personal funds. After one year of operations, the business has accumulated earnings of $750, after owner's withdrawals. Show how the owner's equity of the balance sheet of this business would look after one year.

Encouraged by the success of the venture, the other members of your group decide to join the business. A partnership agreement is drawn up, and each of the new partners contributes $1,000.
After another year of operations, the business has accumulated earnings after withdrawals of $1,950.
What items should be included in your partnership agreement?

What has happened to the $750 of accumulated earnings from last year?

Show the owners' equity section of the balance sheet of the partnership after this latest year of business. What do you have to decide before you can prepare this statement?

Finally, at the beginning of the third year of business, the partners decide they would like the legal protection of the corporate form of organization. By the end of the third year, the business has accumulated $2,350 of earnings. Decide how the corporation will be organized: how many authorized shares, par value, and number of shares to each former partner, now shareholders. Prepare the stockholders' equity section of the balance sheet of your new corporation at the end of Year 3.

And just for the fun of it ...

The ticker symbol of a company is useful to know. Most are fairly obvious, but some are not quite so. Companies get creative, although if you know something about them you see the reason behind the symbol. Below are the ticker symbols of a number of publicly traded companies. Some are companies in this book or your text. Others may be unfamiliar. How many can you identify?

AA	HDI
AMR	HSN
BEAM	HSY
BEAR	JCP
CLD	K
DAL	LEO
DIS	LOTS
EGGS	MCD
ELY	SBA
FLY	TBL
FDX	TOY
GIS	TWX
GPS	WEN
GUSH	WHR
HD	WMT

SOLUTIONS

Multiple choice:
1. (a) 2. (b) 3. (b) 4. (a) 5. (c) 6. (c) 7. (e) 8. (d) 9. (e) 10. (a) 11. (c) 12. (a) 13. (d) 14. (d) 15. (e) 16. (c) 17. (d) 18. (e) 19. (b) 20. (c) 21. (a)

True or false:
22. False. The number of authorized shares is the maximum number of shares the corporation is permitted by its charter to offer for sale.

23. True.

24. True.

25. False. Unlimited liability applies to proprietorships and partnerships, but not corporations.

26. True.

27. True.

28. True.

29. False. Treasury shares are shares that the company has bought back on the open market.

30. False. Without a qualifier, "dividend" means a cash dividend.

31. True.

32. True.

33. False. Restrictions may be disclosed in either the financial statements or in footnotes.

A few words from you ...

37. Cash dividend:

Stockholders' Equity

Common stock $.05 par value	
Authorized 500,000,000 shares; issued 155,733,256 shares	$ 7,787
Additional paid-in capital	240,655
Retained earnings	*1,011,263*
Foreign currency translation adjustment	(8,314)
Restricted stock plan deferred compensation	(48,035)
Total Stockholders' Equity	$ 1,203,356

100% stock dividend:

Stockholders' Equity

Common stock $.05 par value	
Authorized 500,000,000 shares; issued *311,466,512* shares	$ 15,574
Additional paid-in capital	240,655
Retained earnings	*1,019,049*
Foreign currency translation adjustment	(8,314)
Restricted stock plan deferred compensation	(48,035)
Total Stockholders' Equity	$ 1,218,929

two-for-one stock split:

Stockholders' Equity

Common stock *$.025* par value	
Authorized 500,000,000 shares; issued *311,466,512* shares	$ 7,787
Additional paid-in capital	240,655
Retained earnings	1,026,836
Foreign currency translation adjustment	(8,314)
Restricted stock plan deferred compensation	(48,035)
Total Stockholders' Equity	$ 1,218,929

Treasury stock:

Stockholders' Equity

Common stock $.05 par value

   Authorized 500,000,000 shares; issued 155,733,256 shares;

outstanding 145,248,728 shares	$ 7,787
Additional paid-in capital	240,655
Retained earnings	1,026,836
Foreign currency translation adjustment	(8,314)
Restricted stock plan deferred compensation	(48,035)
Treasury stock at cost	*(92,454)*
Total Stockholders' Equity	$ 1,126,475

CHAPTER 12

MEASURING AND REPORTING INVESTMENTS IN OTHER CORPORATIONS

A solid man of Boston.
A comfortable man, with dividends,
And the first salmon, and the first green peas.
Henry Wadsworth Longfellow

OVERVIEW

Corporations invest in the securities of other corporations for a variety of reasons. Often the investment is for a short term, designed to earn a return on idle funds; other investments are for the long term. The latter may be designed to provide the investing corporation with significant influence or control over the other corporation. In this chapter, we will discuss different methods of accounting for these different types of investments.

LEARNING OBJECTIVES

1. Discuss why corporations invest in each other.

2. Compare the available-for-sale and trading securities portfolios.

3. Use the market value method.

4. Record the sale of investments.

5. Use the equity method.

6. Explain the purpose of consolidated statements.

7. Apply the pooling and purchase methods.

8. Prepare elimination entries.

9. Prepare consolidated statements in years after the year of acquisition.

10. Compare the pooling and purchase methods.

CHAPTER OUTLINE

What are the three categories of investment in other companies?

Short term investments are made with the intent of earning a high rate of return on funds needed for operations in the future

 •may be aggressive, high-risk investments, or low risk securities

Long term investments may intend **no influence** on the other company

 •similar purpose to short term investments, but funds are needed for a long term purpose

Long term investments with **intent to influence** another company may be made

 •enhance return on investment

 •combined efforts may be more than the sum of individual efforts

 •only common stock, with voting rights

How does the accounting for investments relate to the type of investment?

Accounting is based on the degree of influence and control

 •**significant influence** is the ability of the investor to have an important impact on the investee

  ◊membership on the board of directors

  ◊interchange of managers

  ◊material transactions

  ◊technological dependency

  ◊at least 20% but not more than 50% of investee's outstanding stock is owned

 •**control** is the ability of investor to determine operating and financing policies of investee

  ◊more than 50% of outstanding stock

Based on degree, accounting method is specified

 •**no significant influence** or control: **market value** method

 •**significant influence**, no control: **equity** method

 •**control**: **consolidated** statements

What is the market value method of accounting for investment?

Market value method is used if under 20% of voting stock is owned, and no significant influence is exercised

- •**trading securities** are held primarily to be sold in the near future
  - ◊held for short-term profit
  - ◊both stocks and bonds
  - ◊always classified as a current asset
- •**available-for-sale securities** are not as actively traded
  - ◊earn a return on funds that may be needed for operations in the future
  - ◊either a current or noncurrent asset, depending on intent of management

Both these types of securities are *listed on the balance sheet at their current market value* as of the balance sheet date, contrary to the cost principle

- •**relevance**: this is the best way to predict future cash flow, which is the purpose of these investments
  - ◊different from most assets, which are held to be used not sold; these securities are held to be sold
- •**measurability**: unlike most assets, there are reliable and accurate ways to determine their current market value

Unrealized holding gains or losses are recorded each time one of these securities is adjusted to its current market value

- •for trading securities, these are included on the income statement
- •for available-for-sale securities, they are reported as a component of stockholders' equity, and not included in net income
- •unrealized gain or loss is the difference between current market value and the value of the asset on the balance sheet on the date of adjustment (*not* the original purchased value, which might already have been adjusted for other gains or losses)
- •any dividends received are recorded as revenue from investments

How are sales of assets from these portfolios accounted for?

The gain (or loss) on the sale of trading securities is equal to the difference between the book value on the sale date and the proceeds from the sale

- •unrealized gains or losses since purchase have already been recognized in income

For available-for-sale securities, unrealized gains or losses must be removed from stockholders' equity and reported on the income statement in the period of the sale of the investments, along with any additional gain or loss on the sale

- •record cash

•debit stockholders' equity for unrealized gain (or credit for loss) to remove the account from equity

•remove securities at their current value from assets

•record total gain or loss on sale

How are investments accounted for by the equity method?

An **equity investor** wants to exert influence without becoming a majority owner

•investment of 20% to 50% of the outstanding stock

•made for long term strategic purposes

•investments *not* reported at fair market value, but at original cost, modified by additions for proportionate share of investee's income

◊original investment recorded at cost

◊when dividends are paid, they are debited to cash and *credited to investment account*

·in effect, a dividend is a return of part of the investment

◊because the investor with significant influence participates in the *process* of earning of income, they also recognize a *share* of that income as an increase to their investment account

·credit to revenue from investments

Why might a company want to gain control over another company?

Vertical integration: a company acquires another at a different level in its distribution chain

Horizontal growth: a company acquires another at the same level

Synergy: two companies together may be more profitable that the sum of the two separately

Diversity: a company lessens dependency on one product, and reduces risks of operation

Special assets: a company may need an asset that another company owns

Undervalued opportunities: acquisition of an unsuccessful company that might return to profitability with capital, or management talent

What is the consolidation method of accounting for a controlling investment?

Consolidated financial statements combine the financial statements of the **parent** company (the investor) and the **subsidiary** (the investee) under the name of the investor

•basically, the statements are added together, account by account

•**intercompany accounts** are eliminated; these reflect transactions between the investor and the investee

◊if they are now one company, these are no longer arm's length transactions (for example, a company would not report a debt to itself)

There are two accounting methods for acquiring a controlling interest: pooling of interests, and combination by purchase

•a **pooling of interests** occurs when a company trades shares of its own stock to owners of another company's stock for their shares in that other company

◊stockholders of acquired company are now stockholders of the acquiring company

◊assets of investee are recorded at their book value, not fair market value

◊pooling is viewed as a joining of ownership interests

◊when statements are consolidated, debts between them (payable for one, receivable for the other) are eliminated

◊investment account on parent's books is eliminated against the paid in capital of the subsidiary

·retained earnings account of subsidiary is not eliminated

·elimination entries are not entered on the books of either, but are done on a **consolidation worksheet**

Reference point: Exhibit 6 in your text illustrates the consolidation of a Parent (P) and Subsidiary (S) company, with the appropriate eliminations, using the pooling of interests method.

•a **combination by purchase** occurs when an investor simply pays cash to the owners of the investee's stock for their shares

◊these former stockholders of the investee will have cash, but no shares in investor

◊assets purchased are recorded at their **fair market value** on the date of the purchase

◊consolidation is similar to pooling of interests

·intercompany debt must be eliminated

·parent's investment account is eliminated against subsidiary's equity accounts, *including retained earnings* ; however, purchase price often exceeds book value of assets

∞increase assets to their fair market value

∞additional excess of purchase price over fair market value is debited to an account called **goodwill,** which can only be recorded when a purchase takes place

∞goodwill is never recorded in a pooling of interests

Reference point: Exhibit 7 uses the two companies you are already familiar with from Exhibit 6. However this time the consolidation is done as a purchase. Review both exhibits carefully, and be sure you understand the differences.

What is different about the consolidation of the financial statements in the years following the acquisition?

In future years the revalued assets and the goodwill have to be depreciated and amortized

•original cost of assets is already being depreciated; only the additional increment for revaluation is depreciated additionally during consolidation

•amortization of goodwill must be recorded over a period of not more than 40 years

How do the purchase and pooling of interests methods affect financial statement analysis?

Return on investment (net income ÷ total assets) measures management effectiveness

•pooling of interests can show higher income

◊no depreciation on asset revaluations, which are not done

◊no amortization of goodwill, which is not recognized

•total assets amount is lower because assets are not revalued and goodwill is not recognized

•higher numerator and lower denominator give a higher ratio

QUESTIONS AND EXERCISES

Multiple Choice:

Choose the best answer to each question below, and circle the letter in front of that answer. More than one answer may be true, but only one best answers the question, so you may have to think over some questions carefully.

1. A company makes short-term investments in order to
   a. have easier access to the cash than long-term investments would provide.
   b. earn a high rate of return on funds that will be needed in the near future for operating items.
   c. accumulate funds for future investments in assets.
   d. minimize investment risk.
   e. have at least a small say in the running of another company.

2. The difference between significant influence and control in a long-term investment is mainly
   a. one of intent.
   b. that for control it is assumed that the investor company owns more that 50% of the investee's stock.
   c. a matter of how much control of the board of directors is achieved.
   d. a matter of how many management personnel it is possible to insert into the investee company.
   e. a question of the type of securities held.

3. When there is neither significant influence nor control, the proper way to measure and report the investment and income from the investment is
   a. the market value method.
   b. the equity method.
   c. the consolidation method.
   d. either (b) or (c).
   e. either (a) or (b) or (c).

4. All nonvoting stock is accounted for under
   a. the cost method.
   b. the equity method.
   c. the market value method.
   d. the investment method.
   e. the consolidation method.

5. Trading securities are held primarily for
   a. influence in the management of another entity.
   b. their desirability to other companies, giving them a guaranteed high resale value.
   c. accumulating funds for the purchase of long-lived assets.
   d. sale in the near future.
   e. trades sometime in the distant future.

6. When a trading security increases in value, it is necessary as part of the closing process to record a(n) _____ on the _____.
   a. income from investments; income statement
   b. income from investments; balance sheet
   c. no entry; the cost principle dictates that assets are held at historical cost until sold.
   d. unrealized holding gain; balance sheet
   e. unrealized holding gain; income statement

7. Available-for-sale securities differ from trading securities in that unrealized gains or losses are recognized
   a. as a separate component of stockholders' equity, not on the income statement.
   b. on the income statement, as opposed to as part of equity on the balance sheet.
   c. only when the security is sold.
   d. differently; losses are recorded, but gains are not.
   e. as other income rather than as regular revenue items.

8. Northeast Retail invested in the common stock of Sarasally Shops at a cost of $250,000. By the end of the year the investment, carried on the books of Northeast as a trading security, was worth $275,000. Shortly thereafter, Northeast sold the shares for $280,000. The entry to record the sale would be

a. Cash   280,000
        Trading securities   250,000
        Gain on sale of trading securities   30,000

b. Cash   280,000
    Unrealized gain on investment 25,000
        Trading securities   275,000
        Gain on sale of investment   30,000

c. Cash   280,000
        Trading securities   275,000
        Gain on sale of trading securities   5,000

d. Cash   280,000
        Trading securities   280,000

e. Cash   280,000
        Trading securities   250,000
        Gain on sale of investment   30,000

9. The equity method presumes an investment was made
   a. to put temporarily excess cash to work in a high-return investment.
   b. as a sinking fund for bond retirement.
   c. for a long-term strategic purpose.
   d. for the purchase of a major asset.
   e. as a first step in purchasing another company.

Use the following information to answer questions 10 – 14. Northeast Outdoor Retail acquired 10,000 of the 40,000 outstanding shares of Charles Camping Equipment on the open market during the Summer of 1995. They are accounting for the investment by the equity method. The $1 par value shares cost $220,000. By the end of 1995 the shares were worth $265,000. Charles earned net income of $1,200,000 during 1995. They declared and paid a dividend of 10¢ per share on December 31, 1995.

10. The entry to record the initial investment would be

   a.   Long-term investment   220,000
             Cash   220,000

   b.   Trading securities   220,000
             Cash   220,000

   c.   Available-for-sale securities 220,000
             Cash   220,000

   d.   Common stock   220,000
             Cash   220,000

   e.   Cash   220,000
             Common stock   220,000

11. As a result of the increase in the market value of the investment by year-end, Northeast would
   a. record an unrealized holding gain on the income statement.
   b. record an unrealized holding gain as a separate item in stockholders' equity.
   c. record the unrealized holding gain as an addition to retained earnings.
   d. make no entry at all.
   e. record the unrealized holding gain as a contra-equity account.

273

12. The entry Northeast would make as a result of the net income earned by Charles would be:

    a.   Cash   300,000
                   Equity in earnings of affiliate   300,000

    b.   Long-term investment   1,200,000
                   Equity in earnings of affiliate   1,200,000

    c.   Long-term investment   1,000
                   Equity in earnings of affiliate   1,000

    d.   Long-term investment   300,000
                   Equity in earnings of affiliate   300,000

    e. No entry would be made for this transaction.

13. Northeast would record the dividend they receive from Charles as

    a. a decrease in the long-term investment account.
    b. an increase in the long-term investment account.
    c. dividend revenue.
    d. an increase in retained earnings.
    e. an increase in unrealized holding gains.

14. Northeast hopes at some point to purchase a controlling interest in Charles Camping. If they achieve this, it would be an example of a

    a. vertical acquisition.
    b. diversification.
    c. horizontal acquisition.
    d. synergy.
    e. a pooling of interests.

15. A pooling of interests occurs when
    a. two companies are in a similar line of business.
    b. more than 50% of a company's stock is acquired by exchanging it for shares of the investor company's stock.
    c. more than 50% of a company's stock is bought for cash.
    d. two companies agree to merge and become one company.
    e. bonds are redeemed for common stock.

16. In a pooling of interests the assets of the acquired company are recognized at _____ and goodwill _____.
    a. their fair market value; is not recognized
    b. their historical cost; is recorded at the excess of cost over value of assets acquired
    c. their fair market value; is recorded at the excess of cost over value of assets acquired
    d. their fair market value; recognition is optional
    e. their historical cost; is not recognized

17. Large Company paid $150,000 cash for 100% of the outstanding stock of Small Company. Small Company's machinery had a book value of $40,000, but an appraisal revealed that the equipment had a fair market value of $50,000. Small Company also had a small but very strong, loyal customer base. For these reasons, Large was willing to pay $150,000 for $128,000 of net book value of stockholders' equity. The amount of goodwill reported on Large's consolidated balance sheet would be
    a. $22,000.
    b. $10,000.
    c. $12,000.
    d. goodwill is not recorded in a combination by purchase.
    e. $128,000.

18. Goodwill is recorded as a(n) _____ , to be amortized over a period not to exceed _____ .

     a. asset; 40 years

     b. liability; 40 years

     c. equity account; 40 years

     d. asset; there is not a limit on the amortization period

     e. asset; 17 years

19. In periods following the acquisition of another company, the presence of goodwill reduces _____ on the consolidated books of the parent company.

     a. cash

     b. total assets

     c. total equity

     d. income

     e. liabilities

20. Return on investment is intended to evaluate

     a. the overall dividend rate of a company's investments.

     b. the effectiveness of the management of a company.

     c. how quickly assets are turned into cash.

     d. how efficiently long-lived assets are being used.

     e. how carefully a company controls expenses.

True or False?

For each of the following statements, place the letter "T" or "F" in the space before the statement to indicate whether you think the statement is true or false. For each false statement, explain why it is false by rewriting it to make it true.

_____ 21. Trading and available-for-sale securities are an exception to the cost principle.

_____ 22. Available-for-sale securities are held primarily for the purpose of selling them in the near future.

_____ 23. Long-term investments with no intent to exert influence are usually less than 20% of the investee's stock.

_____ 24. The market value method is only used when there is no significant influence or control.

_____ 25. In order to have control, a company must acquire more than 50% of another company's stock.

_____ 26. Unrealized holding gains would be reported in the investing section of the statement of cash flows.

_____ 27. A company that acquired 35% of another company's stock would have a choice between accounting for the investment by the market value method, or the equity method.

_____ 28. In simple terms, a consolidation is an adding together of each of the financial statements, line by line, of the parent company and the subsidiary.

_____ 29. In a combination by purchase, the stock of the subsidiary is acquired from its current owners with cash by the parent, or acquiring, company.

_____ 30. For both a purchase and a pooling of interests, the retained earnings of the subsidiary are eliminated on the consolidation worksheet.

_____ 31. The amortization of goodwill has no cash impact, but can have a significant impact on earnings.

A Few Words from You ...

Discuss each of the following questions, applying concepts you have learned in this and other chapters. Support your discussions with calculations where appropriate.

32. **Are these distinctions precise?** You have been told that when a company owns at least 20% (but not more than 50%) of another company, significant influence is presumed. Can you think of an instance where a company could own 20%—or even 25%—of another company and *not* have significant influence?

If the company does not have significant influence, should the investment still be accounted for by the equity method? Explain your answer.

Why would a company put itself into this position?

33. **What does this tell you?** The Vermont Teddy Bear Co., Inc. has the following footnote in their 1993 Annual Report:

> *Marketable Securities*
>
> Marketable securities consist primarily of highly liquid tax exempt mutual funds with maturities of less than one year. Dividend income is accrued as earned. The investments are carried at cost which approximates the market value at December 31, 1993.

Explain the meaning of this footnote. How would these securities be classified and accounted for? What would be Vermont Teddy's reason for having this portfolio?

● 34. **What would be in this portfolio?** General Electric Company (GE), in Footnote 1 to their 1993 Annual Report, says in part,

> Investment securities include both available-for-sale and held-to-maturity securities. Available-for-sale securities are reported at fair value, with net unrealized gains and losses that would be available to share owners included in equity. Held-to-maturity ... securities are reported at amortized cost.

What types of securities would you expect to find in each of the portfolios included in this footnote?

What does fair value mean? What does amortized cost mean? Why are the two types of securities accounted for differently?

●

GE's Footnote 11 says further,

> At December 31, 1993, GECS's investment securities were classified as available-for-sale and reported at fair value, ...

Does this contradict the earlier footnote? Can a security that was once classified as held-to-maturity become available-for-sale? How?

35. **Can the future usefulness change?** Wendy's International, Inc. lists as an asset, "Cost in excess of net assets acquired, net." What is another description of this asset?

● Is it a current or a long-term asset?

What precisely is it?

In a footnote, Wendy's says that this asset is "amortized on the straight-line method over periods ranging from ten to 40 years ..." . The asset is reviewed periodically and "impairments will be recognized when a permanent decline in value has occurred."

What does this footnote mean? Can they change the balance sheet value of an asset? Explain this in terms of what you have learned in this chapter, and also what you know about asset values and depreciation/amortization estimates.

36. **Does Disney "own" Euro Disney?** Most individuals use the term "own" rather loosely when they refer to corporate relationships. Let's explore just one. The Walt Disney Company has an account on its balance sheet called "Investment in and Advances to Euro Disney." Based on this information, is Euro Disney a subsidiary? Explain your answer. What is the corporate relationship?

Footnote 3 in Disney's Annual Report for 1993 states that Disney owns 49% of Euro Disney. What method of accounting for this investment must they use? Why?

In fiscal 1993, Euro Disney incurred a net *loss* of 5.3 billion French francs. What is the impact of this on The Walt Disney company? If you wish to be precise, you can find dollar/franc conversions for September 30, 1993, at the library.

37. **Croissants, anyone?** *The Wall Street Journal* [0] reported that Wendy's International Inc. agreed to buy Canada's No. 2 fast food restaurant, Tim Horton's, in a stock transaction, issuing 16.2 million shares of stock and assuming $125 million of Horton's debt. Horton's focuses on baked goods and coffee, while Wendy's has not in the past had a breakfast menu. Prior to the acquisition, the restaurants shared space in many Canadian locations, and hope to increase this arrangement in the future. The article notes

> Since they launched their restaurant-sharing arrangement, Wendy's and Horton's have opened 13 units in which they share a building but maintain separate staffs and operations. The units cut combined costs by about 25% while boosting traffic for each partner above the average for stand-alone units in Canada.

Explain what kind of business combination—purchase or pooling— this is.

Review the reasons for acquisitions and combinations in your text. Which ones do you see at work here? How will this benefit each business?

---

[0]Murray, Matt, "Wendy's Agrees to Buy Canadian Chain of Eateries in $400 Million Stock Deal," *The Wall Street Journal* , August 9, 1995.

Team up!

Work in teams on the following projects. You'll find that four to five people make a comfortable size, with enough "hands" to share out the work, and generate ideas.

38. **Why did they merge?** Choose two or three recent corporate mergers that interest you. They happen often enough so that you should not have to check far back to find them. *The Wall Street Journal* is a good place to start. Read about the mergers, and then answer the following questions.

Why did the companies merge, or one buy out the other?

Was it a friendly combination?

What kind of business combination was it: horizontal, vertical, synergy? Explain.

How will they account for this combination, as a purchase or a pooling of interests? Explain the accounting implications of their method.

Prepare a short—five or ten minutes—presentation to give to your class on one merger. You might want to take the role of a corporate spokesperson presenting the merger to the press, or employees, or stockholders. Show the reasons for the merger, and the future implications for both companies. What do you hope to accomplish? How will it benefit stockholders? customers? employees?

39. **Do you want to be a corporate Treasurer?** Look in the appendix of your text at the balance sheet of Toys "R" Us. What is their cash balance? Suppose they did not need any of that cash for 30 days. Use the financial pages of your newspaper or the library at your school to research some investment possibilities for that cash. Keep in mind that you have only 30 days, then they want to have the cash back.
How much can you earn on each investment?

How will you account for the investment? the revenue from the investment? the sale of the investment?

Put together in proposal form, as you would for your supervisor in the company, what you believe to be the best combination of investments for the company to use for this cash. Show what they will buy, how much revenue they will earn, and the likely selling price of the portfolio at the end of 30 days.

40. **You're still the Treasurer.** What types of securities would you invest in for each of the following? Why? How would each one be accounted for? Are there any special circumstances or arrangements necessary for any one of them? Explain.

The company's defined benefit pension plan.

A sinking fund for your company's $5,000,000 bond issue.

Your company has bought a 10-acre piece of land in Vermont, and plans to begin construction five years from now on a new corporate headquarters. You must begin the funding plans now.

Your company wants to protect its source of supply of a vital manufacturing component. They now own about 10% of the voting stock of a supplier, and would ultimately like to own about 30%. How would this investment be accounted for now? In the future?

41. **How much difference does goodwill make?** Using your library's resources, find four or five companies who have goodwill in their balance sheet and amortization on their income statement. Explain what this tells you about the companies, in general terms.

For each company, make two return-on-investment calculations. First calculate this ratio as their financial statements stand now. Then, remove goodwill and its amortization from the statements, and calculate return on investment again. Compare the two, and comment on the differences for each company and for all the companies.

And just for the fun of it ...

The following familiar names have one thing in common: they are all wholly, or majority, owned by another company. What does this mean? Even though some are "big" companies, you won't see an individual set of financial statements for them. They are consolidated under another name. Do you know, or can you find, the parent company for each of these?

Banana Republic (clothing)
Brooks Brothers (clothing)
Burger King (restaurant)
Etienne Aigner (small leather goods)
KitchenAid (appliances)
Pizza Hut (restaurant)
Richard D. Irwin, Inc. (publisher of this book)
Ronzoni and San Georgio (pasta products)
Taco Bell (restaurant)
Victoria's Secret (lingerie)

SOLUTIONS

Multiple choice:

1. (b) 2. (b) 3. (a) 4. (c) 5. (d) 6. (e) 7. (a) 8. (c) 9. (c) 10. (a) 11. (d) 12. (d) 13. (a) 14. (c) 15. (b) 16. (e) 17. (c) 18. (a) 19. (d) 20. (b)

True or false:

21. True.

22. False. Trading securities are held for near-term sale.

23. True.

24. True.

25. True.

26. False. Unrealized holding gains, since they are *unrealized* , have no cash impact.

27. False. For ownership of 35% of another company's shares, the company has no accounting choice under normal circumstances except the equity method.

28. True.

29. True.

30. False. Retained earnings are only eliminated for a purchase, not a pooling.

31. True.

CHAPTER 13

STATEMENT OF CASH FLOWS

In epochs when cash payment has become the sole nexus of man with man.

Thomas Carlyle

OVERVIEW

Each year, many companies report healthy profits but file for bankruptcy nevertheless. Some investors consider such a situation to be a paradox, but sophisticated analysts understand how this situation can occur. These analysts recognize that the income statement is prepared under the accrual concept (revenue is reported when earned ant the related expense is matched with the revenue). The income statement does not report cash collections and cash payments. Troubled companies usually file for bankruptcy because they cannot meet their cash obligations (e.g., they cannot pay their suppliers or meet their required interest payments). The accrual income statement does not help analysts assess the cash flows of a company. The statement of cash flows (SCF) is designed to help statement users evaluate a company's cash inflows and outflows.

LEARNING OBJECTIVES

1. Classify cash flows from operating, investing, and financing activities.

2. Convert accrual revenues and expenses to a cash basis.

3. Compare the direct and indirect methods.

4. Define noncash expenses.

5. Compute cash flows from investing activities.

6. Compute cash flows from financing activities.

7. Explain the impact of noncash financing and investing activities.

8. Use a spreadsheet to prepare the SCF.

CHAPTER OUTLINE

What are the classifications within the statement of cash flows?

The statement of cash flows explains how the cash balance at the beginning of the year became the cash balance at the end of the year

- cash includes cash and **cash equivalents**—short-term, highly liquid investments
  - ◊easily converted to cash
  - ◊unlikely to change in value

Statement is divided into operating, investing and financing sections

- cash flows from **operating activities** include items directly related to income from normal operations
- cash flow from **investing activities** is related to the acquisition of long-lived assets and investments
- cash flow from **financing activities** involves inflows and outflows from borrowing, repayment, and capital stock transactions
- noncash investing and financing activities are footnoted or reported in a separate schedule because of their future impact on cash

Two methods are allowed for preparation of the operating section, the direct and the indirect

- the **indirect method** adjusts net income to net cash flow from operations
  - ◊preferred by the vast majority of companies
- the **direct method** reports cash receipts and cash payments that make up operating income
  - ◊preferred by FASB but rarely seen in practice

How is a statement of cash flows prepared under the indirect method?

Certain data are needed:

- an income statement
- balance sheets from the current year and the previous year
- additional operating details to analyze certain accounts

For cash flow from operations, analyze the income statement in terms of changes in balance sheet accounts

•sales revenue is related to accounts receivable, to obtain cash collected from customers

•inventory and accounts payable are analyzed in conjunction with cost of goods sold to obtain cash paid to suppliers

•operating expenses are compared to prepaid expenses and accrued liabilities to derive cash operating expenses

•depreciation expense is added back since it required no cash outlay

Cash flow from investing activities will involve the analysis of long-term asset accounts

Cash flow from financing activities will require analysis of long-term liabilities and owners' equity

How is cash flow from operating activities computed?

Collections from customers depend upon whether accounts receivable has increased or decreased

•accrual revenues + decrease in accounts receivable = cash collected

•accrual revenues - increase in accounts receivable = cash collected

•the rules apply to *all* revenues, both operating and non-operating

•thus, an increase in accounts receivable (sales on credit that did not generate cash) is subtracted from net income on the statement of cash flows

•a decrease in accounts receivable (more cash generated than sales) is added to net income

Cash outlays for expenses depend on increases and decreases in related prepaid expenses and accrued liabilities

•accrual expense + decrease in expense payable = cash paid

•accrual expense - increase in expense payable = cash paid

•decrease in payable account subtracted from net income

•increase in payable account added to net income

Cash paid for cost of goods sold is increased by an increase in inventory

•cost of goods sold + increase in inventory = cash paid for cost of goods sold

•cost of goods sold - decrease in inventory = cash paid for cost of goods sold

◊if there are balances in accounts payable, cost of goods sold calculation requires another step

·cost of goods sold + increase in inventory + decrease in accounts payable = cash paid

·cost of goods sold - decrease in inventory - increase in accounts payable = cash paid

•thus, increase in inventory or decrease in payable subtracted from net income

•decrease in inventory or increase in payable added to net income

Depreciation and other noncash expenses such as bad debt expense are added back to net income

The direct method, in contrast, would adjust each income statement account to a cash basis using the formulae given above

> •NOTE: **SUPPLEMENT** **A** for this chapter shows the preparation in detail using the **direct method**.

Reference point: Review Exhibit 4 in your text to see the direct and indirect methods of preparing cash flow from operating activities contrasted. Computations under the direct method are shown.

How are gains and losses reflected on the statement of cash flows?

Gains and losses must be classified as operating, investing or financing

> •investing and financing items reported on the income statement must be adjusted in the cash flows from operations to prevent double counting
>> ◊subtract gains
>> ◊add back losses
> •total cash collected, not the gain or loss, must be reported on the proper section of the statement of cash flows
>> ◊gain or loss was the difference between net book value and cash collected

How is cash flow from investing activities computed?

Investing activities involve the acquisition or sale of long-term assets

> •cash inflows (disposals) and outflows (purchases) listed separately

Investment strategy reveals to analysts the level of the company's preparation for future growth

How is cash flow from financing activities computed?

Financing activities involve generating capital from creditors and owners

> •involve a review of long-term debt and stockholders' equity
> •dividends on stock are included here

290

•interest, although related to long-term debt, is *not* included in financing, but in the operating activities section

How are non-cash investing and financing activities treated?

Sometimes an asset is purchased in exchange for a note, for example
>•no cash flow effect, but it is a material transaction
>•must be disclosed in either a narrative or a footnote

How can a spreadsheet be helpful in preparing a statement of cash flows by the indirect method?

A spreadsheet is a systematic way of tracking data needed to prepare the statement of cash flows in the complex environment of a large corporation
>•account names are listed on far left of top half of worksheet
>•on far left of bottom half, each statement of cash flows item is listed
>•four dollar columns are needed: beginning balances for balance sheet accounts; debit changes to balance sheet accounts; credit changes to balance sheet accounts; ending balances of balance sheet accounts
>•changes are listed as debits or credits to the top half, with corresponding credit or debit on bottom half recorded as cash inflow or outflow
>>◊thus, to begin the indirect method, net income is shown as a credit change to retained earnings on the top and as a cash inflow opposite the title net income on the bottom half
>>◊an increase in accounts receivable is entered as a debit change to accounts receivable on the top and as a cash outflow entitled accounts receivable increase on the bottom
>•once all entries are complete, the debit column for changes should equal the credit column.

Reference point: Study Exhibit 6 in your text carefully to see the entries corresponding to the previous descriptions of the preparation of the statement of cash flows. Refer to the narrative description of the worksheet entries in the text if any entries are not clear.

SUPPLEMENT A
SPREADSHEET APPROACH TO DEVELOP AN SCF, DIRECT METHOD

How is the spreadsheet for the direct method prepared?

The operating activities section in the direct method shows actual cash flows for each item

- •on left, at top, income statement is copied, with amounts in the two middle (change) columns
- •below the income statement, the balance sheet is copied, with amounts in the first column
- •below the balance sheet, the statement of cash flows titles are written
- •four dollar columns are set up, as in indirect method
- •income statement is recorded as appropriate inflows and outflows of cash
    - ◊credit to revenue is a cash inflow, operating activities
    - ◊debit to expense is a cash outflow, operating activities
- •balance sheet items are analyzed for their impact on cash
    - ◊accounts receivable increase is an outflow (reduces cash) from sales, or collections from customers
    - ◊increase in accounts payable is a cash increase (inflow) opposite payments to suppliers (cost of goods sold)

Reference point: Carefully study Exhibit 8 in your text and refer to the narrative of entries for any that do not immediately make sense.

QUESTIONS AND EXERCISES

Multiple Choice:

Circle the letter in front of the best answer to each of the questions below. More than one answer may be true, but only one best answers the question, so think over the questions carefully.

1. When a company reports healthy net income, that is not a guarantee of future success, because net income is a(n) _____ number, and does not necessarily reflect the company's ability to generate _____ .
    a. accrual; cash
    b. deceptive; sales
    c. estimated; actual income
    d. cash; sales
    e. cumulative; cash

2. The statement of cash flows is divided into the following sections:
    a. current; noncurrent.
    b. inflows; outflows.
    c. operating; investing; financing.
    d. operating; non-operating.
    e. assets; liabilities; equity.

3. Cash flows from operating activities represent
    a. cash inflow from sales.
    b. purchases and disposals of operating assets.
    c. ordinary income items.
    d. cash inflows and outflows from normal operations.
    e. cash income before accounting changes and taxes.

4. Cash flows from investing activities are normally calculated by analyzing
    a. long-term liabilities.
    b. shareholders' equity.
    c. both (a) and (b).
    d. all non-cash assets.
    e. long-lived asset accounts.

5. Included in cash flows from financing activities would be all the following except
   a. the sale of additional shares of the company's stock.
   b. net income for the period.
   c. the payment of a cash dividend.
   d. the repayment of the principal of a bond payable.
   e. the borrowing of cash on a long-term note payable.

6. The purchase of a $475,000 machine in exchange for a 5-year note payable for $475,000 would
   a. be reported in a footnote or supplemental schedule to the statement of cash flows.
   b. not be reported in the statement of cash flows, because it involves no cash.
   c. be included in investing activities as a cash outflow.
   d. be included in financing activities as a cash inflow.
   e. both (c) and (d).

7. The direct method and the indirect method are alternative methods of preparing
   a. the statement of cash flows.
   b. the operating activities section of the statement of cash flows.
   c. the worksheet for the statement of cash flows.
   d. the net income calculation.
   e. cash inflows.

8. A company's sales for its latest fiscal year were $1,500,000, all on account. Beginning accounts receivable for the year were $180,000. Accounts receivable at the end of the year totaled $200,000. Collections from customers were
   a. $1,500,000.
   b. $1,520,000.
   c. $1,480,000.
   d. $1,300,000.
   e. $180,000.

9. Cost of goods sold for a recent year was $450,000. Inventories decreased by $5,000, while accounts payable went from $50,000 at the beginning of the year to $40,000 at year-end. The company's cash payments to suppliers were

    a. $450,000.

    b. $445,000.

    c. $455,000.

    d. $465,000.

    e. $435,000.

10. Refer to the information in question (9). The company's inventory purchases for the year were

    a. $445,000.

    b. $450,000.

    c. $455,000.

    d. cannot calculate from the information given.

    e. $0.

11. A company paid $200,000 cash for salaries for a period when the beginning balance of salaries payable was $5,000. At the end of the period, salaries payable had a balance of $8,000. Salaries expense reported on the income statement was

    a. $203,000.

    b. $200,000.

    c. $197,000.

    d. $208,000.

    e. $192,000.

12. Office supply expense for a particular year was reported to be $322,000. The account prepaid office supplies had a beginning balance of $20,000, and an ending balance of $28,500. Cash paid for office supplies was

    a. $322,000.

    b. $313,500.

    c. $342,000.

    d. $330,500.

    e. $293,500.

13. In a period when interest receivable decreased from $5,000 to $3,000, the company reported interest revenue of $35,000. Cash collections of interest totaled
   a. $33,000.
   b. $35,000.
   c. $32,000.
   d. $37,000.
   e. $38,000.

14. The company's accrued income taxes payable at the end of the year were $30,000. Income tax expense was reported to be $52,000, and payments for the year for income taxes were $40,000. The beginning balance of income taxes payable must have been
   a. unable to calculate from the information given.
   b. $10,000.
   c. $42,000.
   d. $12,000.
   e. $18,000.

15. Depreciation expense for a company was $215,000 for the year. Using the indirect method for cash flow from operations, this expense would be
   a. added back to net income.
   b. subtracted from net income.
   c. not listed on the statement of cash flows.
   d. reported in the investing section as a deduction.
   e. reported in the investing section as an inflow.

16. The company purchased an asset for $90,000. After 3 years, when accumulated depreciation was $52,000, they sold the asset, reporting a gain of $5,000 on their income statement. If they use the indirect method for cash flow from operating activities, in the operating section they would
   a. add $5,000.
   b. add $43,000.
   c. deduct $5,000.
   d. deduct $43,000.
   e. not include this item.

17. Refer to question (16). This transaction should be recorded in the _____ section, as an _____ of $_____ .

    a. operating; outflow; 5,000

    b. investing; inflow; 5,000

    c. investing; outflow; 5,000

    d. supplementary schedule; inflow; $43,000

    e. investing; inflow; 43,000

18. The following information was available for a company for 1995:

	beginning balance	ending balance
Equipment	$9,000	$11,000
Accumulated depreciation, equipment	$3,500	$4,100

The company purchased $3,000 of new assets during the year and sold some old assets for their net book value (no gain or loss). Depreciation expense was reported as $800.

The original cost of the assets sold was

    a. $2,000.

    b. $600.

    c. $1,000.

    d. $200.

    e. $800.

19. Refer to the information in question (18). The accumulated depreciation on the assets sold was

    a. $600.

    b. $200.

    c. $1,000.

    d. $1,400.

    e. $800.

20. Debt with a net book value of $20,500,000 was retired early at a gain of $250,000. The company would report this item on the statement of cash flows in the _____ section as a(n) _____ of $ _____ .

        a. investing; outflow; 20,250,000

        b. financing; outflow; 20,250,000

        c. financing; outflow; 20,750,000

        d. financing; inflow; 20,250,000

        e. financing; inflow; 250,000

True or False?

For each of the following statements, place the letter "T" in the space before the statement to indicate that it is true or "F" to indicate that the statement is false. When you mark a statement "false," rewrite it so that it is true.

_____ 21. When the worksheet method is used to prepare the statement of cash flows, the indirect method is begun by recording a credit to retained earnings for net income for the period, and listing the net income as an inflow on the cash flow section.

_____ 22. On a worksheet, using the indirect method, an increase in accounts receivable would be offset by an inflow to net income.

_____ 23. A debit to inventory on the worksheet (indirect method) would be offset by an increase to net income.

_____ 24. Since bad debt expense is a non-cash item, it is added back to net income when preparing the operating section of the statement of cash flows.

_____ 25. Interest expense related to bonds payable would be reported on the financing section of the statement of cash flows.

_____ 26. The *declaration* of a dividend would *not* be reported in the financing section of the statement of cash flows.

_____ 27. The total increase or decrease for all three sections of the statement of cash flows is equal to the increase or decrease in cash on the balance sheet during the year.

_____ 28. The loss on the sale of a plant asset must be added back to net income when calculating cash flow from operations.

_____ 29. As a general rule, an increase to a non-cash asset is an increase in cash.

_____ 30. As a general rule, a decrease in a liability is an increase in cash.

A Few Words from You ...

Answer each of the following with a short discussion (a paragraph will cover it) of the issues involved.

31. **When is a decrease in accounts receivable not good?** Your text notes that a large increase in accounts receivable could be an indicator of a problem for a company, and must be looked at carefully. What about a *decrease* in accounts receivable? This, on quick analysis, indicates increased collection effort. More collections than sales are being made. Is this always good? Can you think of instances where a decrease in accounts receivable is also an indication of a problem? Explain.

32. **What difference does the depreciation method make?** Charles Co. purchased an asset early this year for $150,000. They are debating about whether to use straight-line or double declining balance depreciation. If they use straight line, their depreciation expense for the first year will be $14,000. If they use double declining balance, depreciation expense will be $30,000. Their revenues for the year were $850,000. Other expenses, all paid in cash, were $720,000.

Which method will produce greater net income?

Which method will produce greater cash flows from operations?

Explain your answers, showing figures to support your explanation.

33. **How do cash flows relate to acquisitions?** *The Wall Street Journal* [1]
reported that Wendy's International Inc. agreed to buy Canada's No. 2 fast food restaurant,
Tim Horton's, in a stock transaction by issuing 16.2 million shares of stock and assuming
$125 million of Horton's debt.

What are the cash flow implications of this transaction?

34. **Why does the FASB like the direct method?** In your text, look over the
operating activities section of the statement of cash flows, prepared in two ways, the direct
and the indirect method. What differences do you observe between the two?

Explain in your own words why you think the FASB might advocate the direct method,
even though businesses in general favor the indirect method as less costly to prepare. What
constituency does the FASB serve? What benefits might they find in the direct method?

---

[1]Ibid.

35. **Can operations pay for expansion?** In the "Year in Review" section of their 1992 Annual Report, McDonald's emphasized in bold type in a contrasting color:

> McDonald's funded capital expenditures with Cash provided by operations in both 1992 and 1991. This trend should continue as a result of reducing development costs, while increasing expansion.

Why is this so important that a company would make particular note of it?

36. **How do they generate and use cash?** Consider two companies in the food business: McDonald's, in the restaurant / food service business; and Hershey Foods, in the food production / manufacturing business.
How do they differ in their ability to turn revenues into cash? Without specific figures in front of you, what could you generalize about the "cash-to-cash cycle" of each?

What can you say about how each company might *invest* cash, that is, what might you find in the capital expenditures of the investing section of the statement of cash flows?

Team up!

Work on the following in teams so that you can help one another find the best solutions.

37. **Worksheet?** Does everyone in your team know how to use a spreadsheet program? This is a good time for everyone to learn, especially if one or two of you already know how. You can teach the rest and sharpen your own skills. Choose one of the problems at the end of the chapter in your text, perhaps one your instructor has already assigned. Instead of doing a handwritten worksheet, set up the worksheet on an electronic spreadsheet. What can you do to make the preparation of the worksheet easier?

38. **Does depreciation have indirect cash implications?** Refer again to question (32) above.

Prepare a simple exhibit with which you could demonstrate the relationship between depreciation and cash flow.

One of the expressed purposes of the ACRS / MACRS tax system was to encourage capital investment by making more cash available to the company.

Again, using simple figures, prepare an exhibit showing the cash implications of the tax tables for a company and how this could aid in capital investment plans.

39. **Can you convert indirect method to direct method?** You have in the appendix to your text the complete financial statements of Toys "R" Us. The company, like most, uses the indirect method to calculate cash flows from operations. Using their statement of cash flows and their other financial statements, can you convert their operating section to the direct method? See how close you can come. (You may not have enough information to do the conversion perfectly.) Which items do you need more information about?

Do you think this ability to convert—albeit roughly—from one version to the other makes the FASB-preferred direct method less of a priority? (HINT: how many readers of the statements can do the conversion?)

40. **20/20 hindsight?** You have been told about the value of the statement of cash flows as an analytical tool. Think of two or three companies that have recently fallen into financial difficulties. Find their statement of cash flows for at least one, preferably two, years prior to these problems. Look carefully at the statement of cash flows. What items can you list that seem to you to be indicators of problems?

And just for the fun of it ...

Cash is cash ... or is it? Many companies today do business in a variety of geographic areas. McDonald's had 4,134 restaurants outside the U.S. at the end of fiscal 1992; Toys "R" Us had 167 international stores at the end of their 1993 year; Wendy's had 4,411 international outlets at the end of 1994. These are primarily "cash" businesses— their customers do not maintain big accounts. But the cash they take in is local currency. These businesses would find it impractical to change prices every time exchange rates fluctuate, so they have to maintain financial arrangements to protect against exchange risk. How much risk is there? Following are a selection of international currencies. Check on three U.S. dollar exchange rates for each: one for a year ago, one for today, and one for a week or so from now, when you are finishing this chapter. How much do the exchange rates fluctuate? How often? Do they all go in the same direction? Do you see any patterns?

Argentina (peso)
Australia (dollar)
Brazil (real)
Britain (pound)
Canada (dollar)
France (franc)
Germany (mark)
Greece (drachma)
Hong Kong (dollar)
India (rupee)
Israel (shekel)
Italy (lira)
Japan (yen)
Mexico (peso)
Saudi Arabia (riyal)
Singapore (dollar)
South Africa (rand)
South Korea (won)
Sweden (krona)
Turkey (lira)

SOLUTIONS

Multiple choice:

1. (a) 2. (c) 3. (d) 4. (e) 5. (b) 6. (a) 7. (b) 8. (c) 9. (c) 10. (a) 11. (a) 12. (d) 13. (d) 14. (e) 15. (a) 16. (c) 17. (e) 18. (c) 19. (b) 20. (b)

True or false:

21. True.

22. False. An increase in accounts receivable would be offset by an outflow to net income—a credit.

23. False. A debit to inventory would be offset by a credit—an outflow—to net income.

24. True.

25. False. Interest expense is reported in the operating section, contrary to what might seem logical to some students.

26. True.

27. True.

28. True.

29. False. An increase to a non-cash asset is a decrease in cash.

30. False. A decrease in a liability represents a decrease in cash.

CHAPTER 14

USING AND INTERPRETING FINANCIAL STATEMENTS

Give us the tools, and we will finish the job.
Winston Churchill

OVERVIEW

Throughout the preceding chapters, we emphasized the conceptual basis of accounting. An understanding of the rationale underlying accounting is important for both preparers and users of financial statements. In this chapter, we introduce the use and analysis of financial statements. Many widely used analytical techniques are discussed and illustrated. An understanding of accounting rules and concepts is essential for effective analysis of financial statements.

LEARNING OBJECTIVES

1. Identify the major users of financial statements and explain how they use statements.

2. Explain the objectives of ratio analysis.

3. List five categories of accounting ratios.

4. Identify and compute 13 widely used accounting ratios.

5. Interpret accounting ratios.

6. Describe how accounting alternatives affect ratio analysis.

CHAPTER OUTLINE

What types of information do users of financial statements want?

Users want information about **past performance**

- this helps evaluate success, and compare the company with others

Users want information about **present conditions**

- in addition to showing past success, this helps predict future prospects

Users want information about the **future**

- users' current decisions cannot change the past

What does an investor consider in evaluating a company?

What is the overall health of the **economy**?

- the company is performing within a general environment: productivity, interest rates, inflation

What is happening within the company's particular **industry**?

- certain events in the economy affect industries differently

What factors are individual to this particular **company**?

- information beyond the financial statements is necessary: visit the company, buy the product, read the business press

What is the company's **strategy**?

- know where they want to go so that you can judge how they are doing in getting there

How do the company's financial **results** look?

- bases for comparison: company's size, prior year's results, other companies
  - ◊**time series analysis**: information for a single company over time
  - ◊**comparison** with other similar companies
    - standard industrial classification codes attempt to group companies within industries

What are ratio and percentage analysis?

A **ratio** or **percent** expresses a proportionate relationship between two different amounts

- no set of ratios is good for everything, and every ratio requires judgment to interpret

Component percentages (or common-size statements) are used to express each item on a particular statement as a percentage of a certain *base amount* (denominator of the ratio)

•base amount for the income statement is sales revenue

•base amount for the balance sheet is total assets

What are the commonly used ratios?

Note that when balance sheet items relating to an instant in time are compared to income statement items covering a period of time, the balance sheet *average amount for the related period* should be used

Ratios are commonly grouped into five categories: profitability; liquidity; solvency and equity position; market tests; miscellaneous

- **profitability** is the measure of overall success

  ◊**return on owners' investment** (ROI_0), or return on equity:

  $$\frac{\text{net income before extraordinary items}}{\text{average stockholders' equity}}$$

  ·reflects return on funds invested by owners

  ◊**return on total investment** (ROI_t), or return on assets

  $$\frac{\text{net income before extraordinary items + interest net of tax}}{\text{average total assets}}$$

  ·reflects return on investments by both owners and creditors

  ◊**financial leverage** $(ROI_0 - ROI_t)$ is the net advantage or disadvantage from earning a different return on owners' investment than on total assets

  ·positive leverage occurs when overall return is higher than aftertax borrowing rate

  ·based on historical values (assets, original investments)

  ◊**earnings per share (EPS)** is net income for a single share of stock

  $$\frac{\text{net income}}{\text{average common shares outstanding}}$$

  ·calculation is complicated by **common stock equivalents**, that is, securities whose value is determined primarily from their ability to be converted to common stock

  ·most relevant figure is the one before extraordinary items, because they are unlikely to be repeated

  ◊**profit margin**, or return on sales is the percent of each sales dollar that is profit

  $$\frac{\text{income before extraordinary items}}{\text{sales}}$$

·does not take into account resources employed, just measures expense control

•**liquidity** measures the ability to meet currently maturing debts

◊the **current ratio** compares current assets and current liabilities on a specific date

current assets
current liabilities

·working capital cushion

·safe level depends on the company's business environment

·it is also undesirable—inefficient—to have too high a current ratio; ties up funds

◊**quick**, or acid test, ratio is more stringent than current ratio

quick assets
current liabilities

·quick assets generally include cash, short term investments, accounts receivable (net)

◊**receivable turnover** measures how many times accounts receivable were recorded, collected, and recorded again during the year

net credit sales
average net accounts receivable

·indicates effectiveness of credit granting and collections

·can be converted to a time basis, **average age of accounts receivable**

days in the year
receivable turnover

·must be evaluated in terms of the particular business for reasonableness

◊**inventory turnover** reflects the liquidity of inventory

cost of goods sold
average inventory

·can be converted, like receivable turnover, to a time basis, **average days in inventory**

days in the year
inventory turnover

·varies greatly depending on the industry

•**solvency** and **equity position** ratios measure the ability to meet long-term obligations

◊equity position is the relative amount of resources provided by creditors and owners

◊**debt to equity ratio** is the proportion of creditor financing to owner financing

> total liabilities
> owners' equity

·debt is risky because there are maturity dates and interest payments to be met, regardless of earnings

·equity has less risk because investments do not have to be repaid, and dividends are discretionary

·debt can provide financial leverage (above) which makes it attractive to have some debt financing

> ∞interest, unlike dividends, is also tax deductible

•**market tests** measure the market worth of a company's stock

◊the **price / earnings ratio** (multiple) relates current market price per share to earnings per share

> current market price
> earnings per share

◊the **dividend yield** relates dividends per share to current market price

> dividend per share
> market price per share

·dividend yields do not tend to be as high as alternative investments; often inversely proportionate to growth potential

•miscellaneous: **book value per share** reveals owner's equity represented by one common share

> total owners' equity applicable to common stock
> common shares outstanding

·generally less than market value

·high ratio of price per share to book value per share is an indicator of good growth potential

What other factors should be considered in analyzing a company?

Some companies have experienced **rapid growth**

> •may obscure the fact that same-store sales are stagnant, or falling, and growth is caused only by opening more outlets

Companies can also be adversely affected by **uneconomical expansion**

310

•good locations are taken, so stores open in less desirable areas

◊average productivity drops

◊measured by sales volume per square foot

Some **subjective factors** must be considered, not found in an annual report

•may require visiting a location

How should ratios be interpreted?

Since rules for computation of ratios do not exist, they should be calculated by the user and not taken from published sources unless it can be determined precisely how they were calculated

•compare with a **standard**, or optimal value

•ratios are averages, and can obscure problems that analysis of underlying figures might reveal

◊sometimes these underlying problems cannot be seen in the published statements

It is necessary to consider the alternative accounting treatments of items in order to understand and compare company results

•review the accounting policies described in the footnotes to the annual report

Evidence suggests that the stock market reacts to information in an unbiased manner: known as an **efficient market**

•generally reacts quickly, so old information is not useful

QUESTIONS AND EXERCISES

Multiple Choice:

Circle the letter of the best answer to each question below. Consider all the choices before you decide, to make sure that your answer is not just a *possible* answer.

1. An example of an economy-wide factor that might affect any company is
    a. a hurricane.
    b. the price of wheat.
    c. gross national product.
    d. increased import tariffs on automobiles.
    e. a winter with relatively little snow.

2. When the balance sheet is expressed in component percentages, all amounts are stated as a percentage of
    a. working capital.
    b. total assets.
    c. cash.
    d. sales.
    e. total equity.

3. Return on investment is a test of
    a. profitability.
    b. liquidity.
    c. solvency.
    d. market strength.
    e. capital structure.

Any calculations of common ratios in the remaining multiple choice exercises will be based on the financial statements for Wendy's International, Inc. & Subsidiaries for 1994, found on the next two pages. Some line items have been condensed to save space where calculations would not be affected.

Wendy's International Inc. & Subsidiaries
Consolidated Balance Sheets
at January 1, 1995 and January 2, 1994
($000)

	January 1, 1995	January 2, 1994
Assets		
Current assets		
Cash and cash equivalents	$ 119,639	$ 71,698
Short-term investments, at market	15,292	40,647
Accounts receivable, net	28,015	27,381
Inventories	19,702	21,478
Other current assets	20,513	17,503
	203,161	178,707
Property, plant and equipment	1,223,687	1,133,780
Accumulated depreciation and amortization	(457,368)	(426,496)
	766,319	707,284
Other assets, net	116,612	110,495
	$1,086,092	$ 996,486
Liabilities and Shareholders' Equity		
Current liabilities		
Accounts and drafts payable	$ 69,845	$ 68,735
Accrued expenses	74,867	63,728
Other current liabilities	62,465	10,806
	207,177	143,269
Long-term obligations	144,860	200,633
Other long-term liabilities	52,557	51,789
Shareholders' equity		
Common stock, $.10 stated value		
Authorized: 200,000,000 shares		
Issued: 101,787,000 and 100,823,000 shares	10,179	10,082
Capital in excess of stated value	171,004	161,238
Retained earnings	503,712	430,866
Translation adjustments	(19)	1,347
Pension liability adjustment	(3,212)	(2,572)
	681,664	600,961
Treasury stock at cost, 29,000 shares	(166)	(166)
	681,498	600,795
	$1,086,092	$ 996,486

Wendy's International Inc. & Subsidiaries
Consolidated Statement of Income
Fifty-two weeks ended January 1, 1995
($000)

Revenues	$1,397,857
Costs and expenses	
Cost of sales	731,691
Company restaurant operating costs	330,480
General and administrative expenses	108,254
Depreciation and amortization	68,070
Interest, net	9,891
	1,248,386
Income before taxes	149,471
Income taxes	52,315
Net income	$ 97,156

Additional facts:

•interest, net = interest expense of $18,720 - interest revenue of $8,829

•price of a share of stock at their year-end, 1994, was $14.38

•price of a share of Wendy's stock, August, 1995, was $17.50

•1994 dividend per share was $.24

---

4. Return on owners' investment for Wendy's is

    a. 14.3%

    b. 15.2%

    c. 9.3%

    d. 10.5%

    e. 10.1%

5. Return on total assets (return on total investment) for Wendy's is

    a. 15.2%

    b. 10.5%

    c. 10.1%

    d. 9.3%

    e. 14.3%

6. Thus, the financial leverage for Wendy's is
    a. 4.7 positive
    b. 4.7 negative
    c. 4.2 positive
    d. 4.2 negative
    e. .9 positive

7. Wendy's profit margin for the year was
    a. 14.4
    b. .65
    c. .105
    d. .0695
    e. .152

8. The current ratio for Wendy's at January 1, 1995, was
    a. 1.02 to 1
    b. 2.68 to 1
    c. .79 to 1
    d. 1.27 to 1
    e. .98 to 1

9. Calculate accounts receivable *turnover* :
    a. .02 times
    b. 7.2 days
    c. 18.2 days
    d. 35.5 times
    e. 50.5 times

10. What is the average days' supply in inventory?
    a. 50.5 days
    b. 2.8 days
    c. 35.5 days
    d. 7.2 days
    e. 10.3 days

11. Equity capital is seen to be less risky than debt capital for the company because
    a. dividends do not legally have to be paid, and it has no "maturity" or pay-back date.
    b. equity does not have to be purchased by investors in such large quantities.
    c. equity can be repurchased by the company more easily.
    d. equity capital distributes ownership of the company more widely.
    e. equity provides more opportunities for financial leverage.

12. Despite the risks of debt financing, companies get significant resources from creditors because of
    a. the benefits of financial leverage.
    b. the ease of selling bonds.
    c. the ability to deduct interest from taxes, but not dividends.
    d. the convertibility of debt.
    e. both a and c.

13. Wendy's total debt to equity ratio at the end of 1994 was _____, representing a(n) _____ in the proportion of debt financing over the course of the year.
    a. .37; decrease
    b. 1.7; increase
    c. .30; increase
    d. .59; decrease
    e. .59; increase

14. Their price / earnings ratio at year-end, 1994, was
    a. 29.3
    b. 6.6
    c. 15
    d. 3.4
    e. 13.7

15. The dividend yield ratio is meant to measure

    a. the average dollar amount of dividends that the company pays.

    b. the return based on the current market price of the stock.

    c. the proportion of earnings per share paid out in dividends.

    d. the proportion of dividends to interest on debt.

    e. the growth in the value of the stock.

16. Wendy's dividend yield as of the end of 1994 was

    a. 1.7%

    b. 59.8

    c. 25%

    d. .24

    e. 21.7%

17. Wendy's book value per share at the end of 1994 (January 1, 1995) was

    a. $10.67

    b. $6.70

    c. $7.53

    d. $6.73

    e. $6.33

18. An increase in total sales may not be an indicator of success if

    a. it is caused by opening more outlets, but same-store sales are decreasing.

    b. accounts receivable is increasing too rapidly.

    c. cost of goods sold is increasing.

    d. collection efforts are not sustained.

    e. operating expenses are increasing.

19. An efficient market

    a. responds immediately to new information.

    b. uses automated systems to update information.

    c. reacts to new information quickly and in an unbiased manner.

    d. takes into account old as well as new information.

    e. processes transactions as quickly as possible.

20. Solvency tests are designed to forecast the company's ability to
   a. avoid bankruptcy.
   b. meet long-term obligations.
   c. meet currently maturing obligations
   d. avoid running short of cash.
   e. both (b) and (c).

True or False?

Mark each of the following statements either "T" or "F" in the space before the statement to indicate whether you think the statement is true or false. As usual, translate each false statement into a true statement.

_____ 21. The past performance of a company can be useful in forecasting future results.

_____ 22. Economy-wide factors affect all companies in the same way.

_____ 23. Time series analysis involves comparing information for a single company for the current and the previous year.

_____ 24. Standard Industrial Classification Codes are a source of potentially comparable companies to be used for analytical purposes.

_____ 25. Return on owners' investment measures net income earned on capital invested by the stockholders of a company, after interest has been paid on debt investments.

_____ 26. Return on total investment, or total assets, is the same as return on owners' investment.

_____ 27. Financial leverage is the advantage or disadvantage the occurs as the result of earning a return on owners' investment that is different from the return on total assets.

_____ 28. Ratios save the analyst time, because as long as the ratios are calculated, the figures underlying them do not have to studied in such great detail.

_____ 29. Book value per share reflects the amount of long-lived assets represented by one share of stock.

_____ 30. The formulae used in calculating the various financial ratios are set by the FASB and can therefore be relied upon to be used uniformly by all companies.

A Few Words from You ...

Discuss each of the following briefly, using calculations to back up your answer where indicated. Many of these questions are based on the Wendy's financial statements found in the Multiple Choice section, and the calculations you did in connection with them.

31. **Who are the comparable companies?** You have been told that analysis of a company's results involves, in part, comparing that company with other similar ones. What kind of company is Wendy's?

From your personal knowledge and experience, can you name some similar companies?

Where could you look for more information? What information might you like to have?

What problems can you anticipate in finding companies to compare with Wendy's?

32. **What does it really tell you?** In question (7), you calculated Wendy's profit margin. Explain in simple terms, to someone who has never heard the term and doesn't know any accounting, what this figure means.

What other information would you like to have in order to decide how good their profit margin is?

What other ratios can be used to test the reliability of the current ratio? Explain.

33. **Do you need to calculate the quick ratio?** Calculate the quick ratio for Wendy's. Is this ratio materially different from their current ratio?

Why might it be less important to have this ratio for Wendy's than for some other companies? What type of company might it be more useful for?

34. **Is this ratio correct?** In question (9) you calculated accounts receivable turnover. Would it be worthwhile to calculate days in accounts receivable? Why or why not?

Is this ratio meaningful for Wendy's? Explain why or why not.

35. **Any surprise?** In question (10) you calculated the average number of days' supply of inventory they have on hand. Was this figure in the range you would have expected for this company? Explain.

What other information might be useful to you in assessing this ratio?

36. **What's the difference?** Explain, again to someone who does not have the knowledge you do, what the difference is between "turnover" and "days' supply."

37. **What are we measuring?** Wendy's includes a number of ratios, for eleven years from 1994 back to 1984, in their Annual Report. They do not calculate debt to equity as you were shown. Instead, they show two other ratios: "long-term debt to equity," and "debt to total capitalization."
Explain and show how you think each one of these alternatives is calculated.

What does each one of these mean? How are they different from debt to equity? Are they measuring something different?

Can you think of instances when you might find one or another more meaningful? In other words, does each have a particular merit of its own? Explain.

38. **How will the purchase change their operating ratios?** In previous chapters [Chapter 12, question (37), and Chapter 13, question (33)] you were told of Wendy's purchase of the Tim Horton's. From just the information you have, how would you expect this to affect Wendy's price / earnings ratio? (Look at the components separately, as well as together.)

What other operating ratios might you expect to change? Explain why.

Team up!

Get together in teams of 3 - 5 members to decide each of the following:

39. **What do common-size statements tell us?** Prepare common-size (component percentages) balance sheets and income statement for Wendy's. You may want to do this right on the page with the statements that were given to you in the multiple choice section.

● What observations can you make about the results of their operations that were not as obvious without converting the statements to percentages?

How might these percentages help in comparing Wendy's to other companies, instead of using dollar amounts?

What other information would you find useful if you wanted to use these component percentages as part of the analysis of the company?

●

40. **Why not do a comparison?** Find one or two companies comparable to Wendy's. Prepare a brief presentation—perhaps to be given to your class—that compares and contrasts the companies. Use the ratios that you consider meaningful or that make a particular point you would like to focus on. (You might want to show what you believe to be the potential impact of their recent purchase, or you may want to focus on inventory management, or use of debt. There are any number of possibilities short of a lengthy "full-blown" analysis.) You could bring some non-financial aspects into your analysis, by doing some site visits.

●

41. **How are we going to remember these?** By this point in the course, you memory has been stuffed with so many facts it cannot handle any more. Then someone presents you with a long list of ratios, which you are expected to memorize. Impossible. You'll jumble them all together on the exam and have a complete disaster on your hands. But some people do remember them, don't they? How? Some are just good memorizers. A lot of the trick is practice: if you do enough problems, you will start to remember the ratios you use. Can you make the job easier? Get your team's heads together. Can you come up with some device—a chart, a picture, a list—to help remember the ratios and their meanings? See what you can do. Then, exchange ideas with the other teams in your class. Between all of you, you will probably have enough ideas to help everyone, no matter how they study. Each of you can choose a method that you think will work for you.

And just for the fun of it ...

Do your courses just end? You go to the last class, you take the final exam, and it's over. Do you ever take a minute to "recap?" Right now, before you go on to other things, sit down and make a list of ten things you learned in this course that you truly believe you will use again in the future, whether in another course, or in an internship you have lined up, or in a job. Be specific (not, "how to read and interpret financial statements"). We hope you have so many items on your list that it is hard to stop at just ten.

SOLUTIONS

Multiple choice:

1. (c) 2. (b) 3. (a) 4. (b) 5. (b) 6. (a) 7. (d) 8. (e) 9. (e) 10. (e) 11. (a) 12. (e) 13. (d) 14. (c) 15. (b) 16. (a) 17. (b) 18. (a) 19. (c) 20. (b)

True or false:

21. True.

22. False. Though "economy-wide" factors seem universal, they may well affect all companies, but not necessarily all in the same way.

23. False. Time series analysis is generally done over a number of years.

24. True.

25. True.

26. False. Return on total investment is calculated as net income with interest expense (net of taxes) added back, divided by total assets. This is not the same as return on equity.

27. True.

28. False. Underlying figures must be considered, since ratios, which are basically averages, can mask underlying factors.

29. False. Book value per share is equal to total stockholders' equity represented by one share.

30. False. The formulae are not standardized, and thus tremendous variation can be found from company to company in precisely how ratios are calculated.

Notes

Notes

Notes

Notes

Notes

Notes

Notes